PARENTING...
A WORK IN PROGRESS

Ellen L. Buikema, M.Ed.

Parenting… A Work in Progress

Copyright © 2014 Ellen L. Buikema

All rights reserved. No part of this book may be reproduced in any form or by any electronic or mechanical means, including information storage and retrieval systems, without permission from the publisher—except by a reviewer, who may quote brief passages in a review—without written permission from the publisher.
For information, contact:
Running Horse Press,
14819 W. Yosemite Drive
Sun City West, AZ 85375

Cover design by Chris Wilke.
Book design and typesetting by Gale Leach.

Published by

Running Horse Press

Sun City West, Arizona

ISBN-13: 978-0-9908979-0-3
ISBN-10: 0-9908979-0-7
LCCN: 2014918567

For information about special discounts for bulk purchases, please contact Running Horse Press at 575-650-2246 or info@runninghorsepress.com.

Dedication

For Ralph, my husband and best friend,
and daughters Laurel and Julia
who always understand their mom.

Parenting... A Work in Progress

Table of Contents

Infants and Toddlers—
Ages Birth through Two Years 1

    Physical Development in Infants and Toddlers 4
        Brain Development.................................4
        Body Growth 6
        Baby Proofing.....................................7
    Motor Skills in Infants and Toddlers 10
        Fine Motor Movements 10
        Gross Motor Movements 10
        Feeding 12
        Choking Hazards..................................15
    Potty Training for Toddlers and Early Childhood...............16
        Are We Ready? 16
        Is It Time?.......................................16
    Cognitive Development in Infants and Toddlers 21
        Toys and Play Materials............................21
        Self-Awareness 24
        Self-Awareness and Language 25
        Self-Regulation...................................26
        Spontaneous Altruism 27
    Language Development in Infants and Toddlers 29
        Interpreting Baby Sounds 29
        Soothe a Crying Infant 30
        Colic 31
        "Why Is My Baby Still Crying?" 31
        From Sounds to Words.............................32
        Second Language Learning 34
    Temperament, Bonding and Attachment in Infants and
    Toddlers..35
        Temperament.....................................35
        Bonding 37
        Attachment......................................37

    Emotional and Social Development in Infancy and Toddlerhood . .41
        Emotional Expression................................41
        Stranger Anxiety 43
        Social Referencing..................................45
    Sleep and Sleep Disorders in Infants and in New Parents 46
        Sleep-Deprived Parents 46
        Postpartum Depression 48
        SIDS - Sudden Infant Death Syndrome 50
    Prenatal Drug Use..51

Early Childhood—
Ages Two through Six 65

    Physical Development in Early Childhood..................67
        Brain Development 67
        Right and Left Hemisphere Specialization 67
    Motor Skills in Early Childhood...........................69
        Children's Art 70
        Activities to Strengthen Hand Muscles:................71
        Letter Reversals 72
    Play and Self-Esteem in Early Childhood 73
        Types of Play 73
        Imaginary Friends..................................74
        Dictated Stories 75
        Mini Dramas.......................................77
        Suggestions to Enhance Make-Believe Play 78
        The Art of Sharing..................................80
        Self-Esteem 80
    Behavior in Public in Early Childhood......................82
        Stores...82
        Restaurants.......................................84
    Discovery Learning in Early Childhood.....................87
        Discovery Learning.................................87
        "There is no screaming in science!" 88
        Early Literacy.....................................89
        Children's Private Speech 90
        Mathematical Reasoning 90

Thinking in Preschool 92
    Time Out 93
    Time to Think About It 93
    "Why do fish swim?" 95
Nutrition in Early Childhood 97
    "I don't want it. I don't like it." 97
    Healthy Snacks 99
Sleep Habits and Problems in Early Childhood 101
    Bedtime Rituals and Other Strategies 101
Explaining Death to Young Children 103

Middle Childhood—
Ages Six through Twelve 111

Physical Development in Middle Childhood 113
    "What happened to you?" 113
    Obesity and Malnutrition 114
    Other Screen-Time Statistics 116
Self-Esteem in Middle Childhood 118
    Preteen Emotions 118
    Developmental Delays 119
    How Schools Can Help 120
Fairness, Friendship, and Love in Middle Childhood 122
    Suggestions to Improve Peer Relations 122
    Let's Be Friends 123
    Love Is in the Air 125
    Love Defined 126
    Build a Better Mattress 127
Parenting Styles in Middle Childhood 128
    Four Parenting Styles 128
    Authoritative Perspective 129
    Authoritarian Perspective 129
    Permissive Perspective 129
    Uninvolved Perspective 130
Home Alone in Middle Childhood 135
    Home Alone Ages by State 135
    The Home Alone Quiz – Is Your Child Ready? 137
    Home Alone Tips for Parents 138
Bullying in Middle Childhood 140
    Suggestions to Help Children Deal with Bullies 143

Parenting... A Work in Progress

Adolescence—
Ages Twelve through Young Adult 151

- Brain Development and Thinking in Adolescence 153
  - "Who are you and what have you done to my child?" ..153
  - "But I can't do math!" 154
  - "Stop, you are making me think too hard.
     My head hurts!" 156
  - "Gotta dance, gotta sing, I have a funny story for you!" 158
  - "Wait, didn't I ask you to clean the bathroom sink
     and throw your dirty clothes into the hamper?" 159
  - The Highway or No Way 160
- To Sleep, Perhaps, To Dream 163
  - "Please, just five more minutes." 163
  - "Earth calling . . . Hey, where did you go anyway?" ..165
  - Why do we dream? 165
- Peer Pressure in Adolescence 167
  - "But it seemed like a good idea at the time!" 167
  - Planning, Impulse Control, and Rational Thinking 168
  - Positive Peer Pressure 169
- Media Influence 170
  - "But I'm supposed to look like them." 170
  - Body Image 171
  - Eating Disorder - Bulimia 171
  - Health Consequences 172
  - Attractiveness Through History 173
  - How Parents Can Help 174
- Social Media in Adolescence 175
  - Cyber Life Calling 175
- Cyber Bullying in Adolescence 177
  - A Successful School Approach 179
  - Warning Signs That Someone May Be the Victim of
     Cyber Bullying 180
  - How Parents Can Help: 180

**Siblings and Divorce—
Infants through Adolescence** **187**

    Siblings 187
        Bringing Home Baby............................187
        Preparing Siblings for the New Baby 188
        Sibling Rivalry 189
    Divorce 192
        Behavior Changes 192
        Children's Positive Adjustment 194
        "What I Need From My Mom and Dad":
            A Child's List of Wants 196
        Therapy Types...................................197
        Children's Books on Divorce 198

Conclusion **203**

Acknowledgements

This book would not have been possible without the encouragement of family, friends, and members of the West Valley Writer's and Northwest Valley Writer's Critique groups.

I am grateful to many classroom teachers with whom I have worked. In particular Ashley Britt, Linda Currer, Laura Davenport, Carol Erkman, Teresa Hess, Eva Marquez, Ami Montoya, Julie Potter, Diane Quinn, Irma Ruiz, Sally Slonina, Kim Tibbs, and Jennie Wirth, and I thank you for generously sharing your knowledge about working with children.

Thank you to Tamarack Country Day School, Mundelein Cooperative Preschool, College of Lake County, Waukegan Public Schools, Saddleback Valley Unified Schools, Las Cruces Public Schools, and Dysart Unified Schools for enhancing my ability to work with children.

I wish to thank John Toma, Ph.D. in Neuropsychology, John Ford, DDS, Janet Benoit, RN, Ami Montoya, MA in Special Education/Deaf-Hard of Hearing, and Daniel Buikema, MS in Counseling, for their professional advice; Suzanne Buikema, Carol Pusateri Ross, and Brandy Stanford for their heartfelt parent interviews.

I am forever grateful to my many students. You have taught me more than you will ever know.

A special thank you to:

...my beta readers—Teresa Hess, Julie Potter, and Sally Slonina;

...Ekta Garg (thewriteedge.wordpress.com), my editor, for your patience, insights and comments on the manuscript;

...Gale Leach (www.galeleach.com) for guiding me through the art and science of publishing and patiently answering my many questions.

Parenting... A Work in Progress

Disclaimer

The information provided in this book is designed to provide helpful information about the subjects discussed. This book is not meant to be, nor should it be, used to diagnose or treat any medical or psychological condition. For diagnosis or treatment of any medical problem, consult your own physician. The author and publisher are not responsible nor liable for any damages or negative consequences from any action or application by any person reading or following the information in this book. The stories and their characters are fictional with the exception of those who have given permission to use their names. Any likeness to other persons, either living or dead, is strictly coincidental. References and other readings are provided for informational purposes only and do not constitute endorsement of any websites or other sources. Readers should be aware that the websites listed in this book may change.

Trademarks

The following trademarked items are referenced in this book:
- Facebook is a registered trademark of Facebook, Inc.
- Hooters is a registered trademark of Hooters of America.
- Infant Massage USA is a registered trademark of Infant Massage USA.
- Kermit-the-Frog, Miss Piggy, Mary Poppins, and Winnie-the-Pooh are registered trademarks of Walt Disney Co.
- My-Little-Pony is a registered trademark of Hasbro, Inc.
- Quaker Oats is a registered trademark of Quaker Oats Company.
- LinkedIn is a registered trademark of LinkedIn Corporation.
- Pinterest is a registered trademark of Pinterest, Inc.
- Twitter is a registered trademark of Twitter, Inc.
- YouTube is a registered trademark of Google Inc.

All other trademarks and registered trademarks are the property of their respective owners.

Preface

When pregnant with my first child, I felt confident in my readiness to be a mom. I read about what to expect during pregnancy and how the baby develops. I remember comparing babies *in utero* with a friend who was also pregnant for the first time. She was further along than I. She told me that at this stage my baby probably looked like a lizard. That comment did not go over well.

Truthfully, my first child was a mystery to me. She cried all the time, so much so that one of my brothers called to ask if she was still screaming. When hungry she let everyone on the block know it, or at least it seemed that way. I needed to learn to relax, despite my fear of doing the wrong thing and ruining my child for life. I worried all the time.

Parenting did not come naturally to me. I had always gotten along well with other people's children, but they went home. My own child was already home. What to do?

I wrote *Parenting...A Work in Progress* to share parenting experiences, talk about the science of why children do the things they do, and offer suggestions to guide you from newborn to adolescence, all while helping you keep your sanity.

Parents do not have to be perfect. Perfection is annoying and an impossible standard to meet. Parents *do* need to understand why their children are the way they are. Learning the reasons behind behavior makes it easier to have patience, a key element of good parenting.

This book is for those who are interested in learning why children do and say the things they do. It is divided into five sections:
- Infants and Toddlers—birth through age two years;
- Early Childhood—ages two through six;
- Middle Childhood—ages six through twelve;
- Adolescence—ages twelve through young adult ;
- Divorce and Siblings—infants through adolescents.

Parenting... A Work in Progress

The five sections cover elements of physical, cognitive, and social-emotional growth. In addition, each section contains chapters especially pertinent to that particular age group. Infants and Toddlers discusses potty training, temperament and attachment, prenatal drug use, and sleep disorders in children and new parents. Early Childhood covers play, discovery learning, behavior in public, nutrition, and teaching children about death. Middle Childhood includes self-esteem, parenting styles, love and friendship, and bullying. Adolescence covers organized thought, dreaming, peer pressure, eating disorders, and social media. The information in the fifth section containing two chapters, "Divorce" and "Siblings," pertains to all age groups. References for further reading and more information are listed at the end of each section.

Parenting... A Work in Progress is the compilation of thirty years of experience—mine and that of parents and professionals who have graciously lent their thoughts and trials of parenting, the hardest job you'll ever love.

Section 1

INFANTS AND TODDLERS—
AGES BIRTH THROUGH TWO YEARS

Newborns come into the world with reflexes that protect and assist them. Most reflexes, except blinking and sucking, which are permanent, disappear completely by four to six months. Stroking a baby's cheek will cause the infant to turn his head towards the touch. This rooting reflex helps the baby find the nipple. Other reflexes help the baby cling (Moro reflex), grasp (Palmar reflex), reach (Tonic neck reflex), step, and swim.

Newborns sleep anywhere between sixteen and twenty hours per day and stay awake from one to two hours at a time. Infants sleep a total of thirteen to fifteen hours including naps.

Babies cry and use body language to communicate. With time and patience, parents will learn their child's cries and interpret meaning from the sounds. Babies cry for a reason. Always. Letting the baby "cry it out" is no longer considered a sound idea. When babies cry they are communicating a need: hunger, pain, discomfort, exhaustion, or lack of stimulation.

Most newborns can hear, taste, touch, smell, and see. These senses trigger emotions that help develop memory and help us navigate through life. At birth, vision is the least developed sense. The newborn's clearest vision is the distance between mother's breasts and her face—about eight to twelve inches. Infants love to look at faces, especially their parents' and their own. Sharp contrasts in color, especially black and white like a panda bear, are easiest for young infants to see.

Newborns become infants at three months. For optimal development, an infant's environment should stimulate all senses. Talk to them. Play music, sing, and dance. Children are not critical when singing is off key. Begin reading to children early. Holding the child close while looking at books together may help create an early love of reading and increase the bonds between the parents and the child.

Touch is vital for physical and emotional development (Berk, 2002). A study of preterm infants who were massaged gently several times a day in the hospital gained weight faster, and after a year were advanced in cognitive and physical development compared to preterm infants who were not massaged (Field et al., 1986).

Toddlerhood begins around twelve months. Toddlers love to take things apart, bang items together, and drop things from all heights. Both of my children, after grabbing hands full of their first birthday cake, dropped the cake and plate onto the floor, then stared at it as if willing the cake to float back up. When toddlers deliberately act on items in their immediate environment, they discover their movements have a predictable effect. This is how they begin to develop a sense of self as separate from their parents and other caregivers, which begins about age fifteen months through around two years (Toma, 2014).

Toddlers take a long time to feed themselves. A relaxed meal is nearly impossible with a strict time limit and may lead to poor digestion for everyone. In any interaction with children, try not to multi-task and allow plenty of time.

Toddlers often show spontaneous altruism. Eighteen-month-old children can infer a goal and help. The child might pick up something dropped by an adult and give it back without prompting. Toddlers are willing to help without need of reward.

At around eighteen months, children become self-aware. A toddler will look at a mirror and know that she is the "baby" in the mirror. Part of growing up is the struggle to be independent. Children and parents will not always share the same desires. The combination of self-awareness and the desire to be separate from parents' influence causes the increasing use of the word "No."

Self-regulation, the ability to control bodily functions, pay attention, concentrate, and control emotions without outside influence, begins around eighteen months and continues to develop to about age five years. Children who learn to self-regulate tend to have an easier time in school, making friends, and dealing with life adjustments (Bronson, 2000).

Understanding language comes before the ability to speak. As the facial and mouth muscles mature, children are able to make sounds that mimic beginning speech, first cooing around two months, then babbling at four months. First words, which begin about twelve months, are generally names of people important to the child, favorite toys, and "bottle" if bottle fed. At eighteen months, children often communicate using two-word phrases. By two years of age, children begin to increase the length of sentences.

Parenting... A Work in Progress

Physical Development in Infants and Toddlers

Brain Development

A baby's brain contains billions of nerve cells, or neurons, storing and transmitting information. The neurons have tiny gaps between them called synapses. Chemicals released by the neurons cross the synapses to send messages to each other. Nerve cells that receive stimulation from the environment make more synapses. Those neurons that are seldom stimulated lose their synapses. This is called synaptic pruning.

> Tamara Sanford's pregnancy went without a problem, but both Tamara and her obstetrician were concerned. During the first trimester, Tamara developed rubella—German measles. This infection can cause the baby to develop cataracts, hearing impairment, mental retardation, seizures, and microcephaly (a smaller than normal head).
>
> "Dr. Green, what can I do?"
>
> "Well, Mrs. Sanford, you've done everything you can. You never miss an appointment, have been taking all your prenatal vitamins, and are careful with what you eat and drink. We can only wait and see."
>
> Tamara delivered a beautiful baby boy. She named him Samuel. Right after his birth, a pediatrician at the hospital used a "red reflex" test to check for cataracts. All looked well. By his one-month well-baby checkup, Samuel appeared to be developing normally with the exception of minor hearing loss. The family

Infants and Toddlers—Ages Birth through Two Years

> pediatrician, Dr. Hernandez, repeated the "red reflex" test.
>
> "Mrs. Sanford, it appears that Samuel has clouding on the lenses of both eyes. He has cataracts. It's not affecting him now, but we really should get the cataracts removed before he's two months old. If we wait longer than that, Samuel may have little or no vision."

If one sense is not used, the area of the brain responsible for that particular sense is "rewired" and used to assist the other senses (Karns et al., 2012). If Samuel lost his sight during infancy, the area of his brain responsible for sight would be "pruned" and rewired to enhance the other sensory areas of his brain.

Children have no vision for details until about three months. Pastel colored toys will not be appreciated, but toys with strong contrasts, like panda bears, are easier for a very young child to focus on. Infants use other senses to differentiate people and environmental events. The children's environment should stimulate sound, smell, and texture for all their senses to develop to their fullest (Toma, 2014).

During the first two years of life the brain develops dramatically, growing from 30 percent of adult weight at birth to 70 percent by age two (Berk, 2002). Much of that growth consists of glial cells that insulate the neural fibers with a fatty protein called myelin. This insulation allows for a smooth information transfer from nerve cell to nerve cell, which is how the brain communicates with the rest of the body.

If myelin is damaged, misfires occur, similar to what happens when there are holes in electrical insulation. The signals between the brain and other parts of the body are interrupted, affecting the senses, the ability to think, and physical movement.

The final area of the brain to develop is the frontal lobe, responsible for thought and consciousness. Myelin begins to form there at two months of age, but the area is not fully insulated until ages twenty to thirty years (Wolfe, 2011). Experience determines how we are "wired." Attending to your children helps to develop and stimulate a better brain.

Body Growth

The body grows in little spurts during the first two years of life. Just before a growth spurt, children are cranky and hungry. Baby fat helps the infant keep a constant body temperature. During the second year, the extra fat is not necessary and the baby begins to slim down.

At birth the baby's skull is separated by six gaps, or soft spots, called fontanels. These gaps allow the baby's skull bones to overlap during delivery. The gaps close during the second year, forming seams that expand to allow for brain growth. In some unusual cases, a baby may be born without fontanels. This poses a danger to the mother and child during delivery. A Caesarean section may be necessary for the safe delivery of the child. The baby's head may be too large if the skull bones are unable to overlap (Cincinnati Children's Hospital Medical Center, 2012).

> Mrs. Leighton looked at her newborn son as she cradled him in her arms. "There's something wrong with my baby's head. It just looks . . . I don't know . . . wrong."
>
> The labor and delivery had taken a long time. The doctor, concerned with the well-being of both mother and child, performed an emergency C-section to facilitate the birth.
>
> Harold put his arm around his wife's shoulder. "Dear, you are just exhausted. I'm sure our little guy is fine. He took a beating trying to get into the world. I read that babies often have heads that look misshapen. All those babies in the nurseries have cute little hats on so the parents don't freak out."
>
> Harold Leighton bent down, gently kissed his wife on her forehead, and placed his baby boy in the bassinet.
>
> Later in the month, the Leightons took little Lawrence in to see the doctor. Lawrence cried all the time, and both mother and father were worried and sleep deprived.

> The pediatrician was concerned. "Lawrence does not have as many soft spots as he should. He may need to have surgery to give him an artificial seam in his skull so his brain has room to grow. Your little guy probably has a whopper of a headache!"
>
> The surgery was successful. Lawrence became a much happier baby.
>
> The surgeon showed a sliver of bone removed from Lawrence's skull. There, on the underside of the skull bone, was an impression of brain. Lawrence's brain had pushed itself directly against the skull, causing pressure headaches.

Baby Proofing

As babies begin the second half of their first year, they are better able to move around in their environment. Parents need to make the home safe for their infants. Areas of the home and items within it, which adults might not deem dangerous, may be hazards for the young child. The National Safety Council suggests the following:

To avoid suffocation and choking:

- Do not place infants on soft surfaces.
- Make babies sleep on their backs.
- Crib bars should be no further apart than 2-3/8 inches.
- Keep crib clear of large stuffed toys and pillows.
- Do not allow infants to play with ribbons, strings, or cords.
- Keep the crib away from windows and window pull cords.
- Use safety gates, with small openings, at the top and bottom of staircases.
- Avoid any food that could lodge in a child's throat. (See choking hazards in motor skills chapter)
- Never let children eat while lying down.
- Keep surfaces free from small objects. Young children explore everything with their mouths, including deflated or pieces of balloons, which may be fatal.

Parenting... A Work in Progress

To avoid falls and burns:
- Set the hot water thermostat no higher than 120 degrees.
- Check temperature safety of children's bath using elbow or wrist.
- Store matches out of reach. Do not allow children to see you use them. They learn quickly.
- Do not hold anything hot while holding a child.
- Stow electrical cords in a safe place.
- Use safety plugs in electrical sockets.

To avoid drowning:
- Never leave a child alone in the bathtub or pool, even for a minute. Let the phone ring. You can always call back.
- Don't leave a small child alone with any container of liquid.
- According to the National Safely Council, the typical drowning victim is a boy between one and three years old who was in the pool when no one realized he was there.
- Do not rely on flotation devices to keep a child afloat.
- Keep toys away from pool area.
- Teach children to swim.
- Learn first aid.

Get on your hands and knees and crawl around the house. Looking at the room from the child's perspective helps parents see what the child will find tempting to pull or climb. For the infant and toddler, all learning is experiential. Let them learn in safety.

According to the American Academy of Pediatrics, keep infants and toddlers safe by doing the following:
- Match the toy type to the child's age and abilities. Some toy types and ages are listed in the chapter on "Cognitive Development" in "Infants and Toddlers."
- Inspect toys for sharp edges, their ability to shatter, and small parts that might accidentally be swallowed.

Infants and Toddlers—Ages Birth through Two Years

- Avoid cord-activated toys and toys to be attached to the crib or playpen; they pose danger of strangulation. The toy could come lose and may hit or be swallowed by the child.
- Remove crib gyms and mobiles when the infant begins to get on hands and knees.
- Do not allow infants and toddlers to play with balloons, which easily become stuck in the throat causing suffocation.
- Close off water areas, including toilets. It only takes a small amount of water and little time to drown.
- Lock up all toxic substances, including medicines and makeup.
- Use safety plugs in all outlets.
- Keep cords out of reach.
- Remove all unstable furniture.
- Never leave a child unattended.
- Use car seats correctly. According to the National Highway Traffic Safety Administration approximately 80 percent of child safety seats are incorrectly installed and will not protect the child as intended in an accident. Technicians trained to examine child passenger safety seats can ensure that they are installed correctly. Car seat clinics are available at some stores. Police and fire departments have people certified to install car seats who will help free of charge.

Parenting... A Work in Progress

Motor Skills in Infants and Toddlers

Fine Motor Movements

Newborn babies swipe at objects. They cannot control their arms and hands. Around three months of age, infants' movements become deliberate. By seven months, a baby may reach for an object using one arm rather than extending both (Fagard & Pezé, 1997). Hand dominance is the preference of one hand to perform gross and fine motor activities. Whichever hand the baby chooses to extend is often the dominant hand. Left or right hand dominance can be tested with finger food during later infancy or toddlerhood. Some children show no preference for left or right, known as being ambidextrous. Athletes often have no hand dominance. Forcing a child to use a particular hand may contribute to learning delays.

Typically, children display fine motor skills in this order:
- Pre-reaching or swiping
- Reaching with the whole hand
- Moving an object from one hand to the other
- Grasping with thumb and fingertips

Gross Motor Movements

Fine motor movements use smaller muscles, like the muscles in hands, while grasping and holding on. Gross motor movements use large muscles for crawling and walking. "Motor control of the head comes before control of the arms and trunk, which comes before control of the legs" (Berk, 2002, p. 190).

Usually children display gross motor skills in this order:

Infants and Toddlers—Ages Birth through Two Years

- Hold head up
- Lift head and chest up by pushing up on the arms
- Roll from side to back
- Roll from back to side
- Sit alone
- Crawl
- Pull self up to stand
- Cruise
- Stand alone
- Walk alone

When children learn to crawl, they get on both hands and knees and make rocking movements. Sometimes when children rock to move forward, they move unintentionally in a different direction.

> I knew the day was coming. Baby Laurel rocked back and forth on her knees on the living room floor. Smokey, our family cat, glanced at Laurel, and turned her head in disinterest. Laurel, intent on reaching Smokey's furry tail, rocked a bit faster on her hands and knees. She moved backwards.
>
> Laurel howled. Smokey ran for the safety of my lap, only to bounce off my leg as I walked across the living room floor to soothe her. She would grab that tail soon enough.

Moving in an unexpected direction frustrated my daughter. With practice children eventually move forward.

Not all children crawl. Sometimes a child sits up on her bottom and scoots across the room. Others "army crawl," where the baby moves in a crawl pattern with the tummy on the floor, or elbows or hands moving along the floor, legs dragging behind. Babies who army crawl may need to strengthen their cores. Encourage the baby to crawl over a pillow, cushion, or a person to get to a desired item. This will tire the baby, so expect him or her to drop on the tummy in fatigue. The baby's core will strengthen, and army crawling will lessen.

Feeding

Solid food given too early increases the risk of food allergies. The infant's digestive tract is immature and only capable of digesting breast milk or formula.

When food is introduced to an immature digestive system, some of the components of that food leak from the digestive tract into the body. This can cause possible sensitivity to that food, and the sensitivity may become an allergy. Pediatricians and nutritionists suggest waiting at least six months before adding finger foods to the infant's diet and adding them one at a time to test for sensitivity. There is evidence that breast feeding for at least the first four months prevents or delays some allergies (Greer et al., 2008).

Studies have shown that the likelihood of breast cancer decreases in women who breastfeed their babies for more than six months. Countries like Japan, where the majority of mothers breast feed their infants, have a much lower incidence of breast cancer than other developed nations (Brey et al., 2004). The findings of the United Kingdom National Case-Control Study, as well as a number of other investigations, indicate a significantly lowered risk for breast cancer among young women with increasing duration of breast feeding or with the number of children breast-fed (Oxford Journals, 2000). Note, however, that a change to a more western diet negated some of the protection provided from breastfeeding.

By nine months of age, babies have developed the fine motor skills necessary to pick up small pieces of food and feed themselves.

Food that is bite sized and easily handled and eaten by a baby can be considered a finger food. Children have a strong interest in feeding themselves finger foods. O-shaped toasted oat cereal and bits of banana are easy for children to gum to a proper consistency for swallowing.

When you feed a child baby food from a spoon, he will want to grab that spoon and feed himself.

> Andre sat in front of his son's highchair. Little Michael, twelve months old, opened his mouth wide. "Here comes more applesauce for my big boy!"

> Michael bounced his fists on the tray of his highchair, giggled, and smiled at his daddy. Before Andre could get the applesauce into Michael's mouth, Michael reached out with his chubby hand and grabbed the spoon from his father. Still not quite coordinated enough to get the spoon where he wanted, he proceeded to feed his hair and throw the spoon on the floor. Michael looked down at his spoon as if he wondered why it stayed there and didn't come back up—early trials in physics.
>
> Before Michael had time to cry, Andre deftly picked up another spoon and fed his son more applesauce. "Here you go, little man. Who loves his applesauce? You love your applesauce." This dance of eating and grabbing spoons continued for five spoons, and all five were on the floor by the end of the meal. One spoonful made it to Michael's mouth by his own hand. Applesauce was all over daddy and son, but the interaction was lively and without pressure.

When children realize they are independent of their caregivers, they notice they have an effect on their immediate environment. They move and drop items with purpose (Toma, 2014).

> My children were huge fans of mashed fruit mixed in yogurt—nutritious and easy, always a plus in my household. Laurel, my mural artist (for more on this see Motor Skills in Early Childhood), sat in her walker that had a large tray attached to the front, handy for food or toys. Adept at using a spoon, she ate blueberry yogurt from a small, unbreakable bowl.
>
> I turned around to stir a large pot of spaghetti sauce. It couldn't have been more than a minute. Laurel was very quiet. That should have been my first clue. I turned back to see my daughter covered in blueberry bliss. Apparently she'd decided eating with fingers would be faster, and finger painting the wall behind her—wow,

Parenting... A Work in Progress

> that was just great fun!
>
> Instead of yelling, which was the first thing that came to mind, I took a deep breath and picked up my blue-berried baby. Off we went to take a shower.
>
> Yogurt on her clothes
And in her hair
Yogurt, yogurt everywhere
>
> My daughter in her exploration of food experimented with different modes of feeding herself. I learned not to multi-task when my children were eating.

Safe Finger Foods

KidsHealth.org suggests some safe finger foods:

- Low-sugar cereal
- Small pieces of lightly toasted bread or bagels (spread with vegetable puree for extra vitamins)
- Small chunks of banana or other ripe peeled and pitted fruit, like mango, plum, pear, peach, cantaloupe, or seedless watermelon
- Small cubes of tofu
- Well-cooked pasta spirals cut into pieces
- Very small chunks of soft cheese
- Chopped hard-boiled egg
- Small pieces of well-cooked vegetables, like carrots, peas, zucchini, potato, or sweet potato
- Small well-cooked broccoli or cauliflower "trees"
- Pea-size pieces of cooked chicken, ground beef or turkey, or other soft meat

Self-feeding gives children some independence, which by two—the age of everything "no"—is important. All foods should be cleared with the pediatrician before introducing them to children. Introduce foods one at a time, and wait a few weeks before introducing the next new food. Keep a goodly number of spoons nearby at mealtimes. You will go through many of them.

Choking Hazards

Parents and caregivers can help prevent choking by supervising the baby during eating. According to KidsHealth.org, the following finger foods are considered choking hazards:
- Pieces of raw vegetables or hard fruits
- Whole grapes, berries, cherry or grape tomatoes (instead, peel and slice or cut in quarters)
- Raisins and other dried fruit
- Peanuts, nuts, and seeds
- Peanut butter and other nut or seed butters
- Whole hot dogs and kiddie sausages (peel and cut these in very small pieces)
- Untoasted bread, especially white bread that sticks together
- Chunks of cheese or meat
- Candy (hard candy, jelly beans, gummies, chewing gum)
- Popcorn, pretzels, corn chips, and other snack foods
- Marshmallows

Feeding is one event where motor development is easy to observe, particularly for fine motor skills. Small muscle movements become more refined and children grasp small pieces of cereal or spoons with ease, no longer swiping at interesting objects.

Potty Training for Toddlers and Early Childhood

Are We Ready?

Potty training is a major step for children and parents. Success in this monumental endeavor will require a healthy dose of humor and possibly the patience of a stone statue. Many children show an interest in using the potty by age two. Others show no desire until it is time to go to preschool.

Don't rush into potty training; it causes stress for both parents and children. Children become ready to use the potty at different ages because of a difference in awareness of their body functions and muscle maturity. Potty training begun too early will take longer to accomplish.

Is It Time?

Think about the following questions.
Does your child:

- show an interest in the potty chair?
- want to wear "big boy" or "big girl" underwear?
- follow directions?
- let you know when he is ready to go?
- seem ready to pull down and pull up his pants?
- dislike soiled diapers?
- sit on and get up from a potty chair unassisted?
- stay dry for at least two hours at a time during the day?

If you answered "yes" to most of the questions, your child is probably ready to begin potty training. If many answers were no, consider waiting. Forcing the issue or pressuring the child too soon will only make using the potty a battle.

Infants and Toddlers—Ages Birth through Two Years

Transitions in the family, such as a new baby or moving to another home, put stress on everyone in the household. Postpone potty training if big changes are planned for the near future.

Sometimes transitions are unavoidable.

> A job change required a long distance move. Austin, the three year old in this particular family, had just finished potty training. He still needed a pull-up at night but was completely potty trained during the daytime. Neither parents nor grandparents considered the ramifications for the youngest in the family.
>
> At the new house Austin refused to move his bowels. The body can hold solid waste for a limited number of days. On day three, Austin stood in front of the toilet, legs crossed, on his tippy-toes, desperately trying to hold in his poo. It was his poo, and he wasn't going to give it up. Finally, Austin could no longer will his body to hold it. With much straining, he delivered an enormous bowel movement.
>
> Austin was anal retentive because he felt a lack of control. His life was changed dramatically by the move. Since he couldn't control what the adults in his life were doing, he attempted to control what he could.

Parents might give their child a small job to help them become involved with the move. The child might be given a box for his or her toys. Give the child a choice of two or three possible places in the new bedroom for the toys' new home. Let the child know he or she is important by allowing some decision making.

> Nancy, twenty three months old, had watched her three-year-old friend, Fay, use a potty chair and seemed interested in trying to use it. Nancy's parents purchased the same potty chair and placed it on the bathroom floor near the "big person" toilet. Nancy bobbed her knees up and down when she saw her new potty.

Nancy's father, George, squatted at eye level with his daughter. "Go ahead, Nancy. Sit down on the potty like a big girl. Here, let me open the lid for you."

Nancy grabbed the lid before George could reach it. "No. I do it."

Nancy's mother, Grace, joined them.

"Well, Mommy, our Nancy certainly has the N-O word down."

Grace put her arm around George's shoulder. "Do you think it's because she hears it so much? Nancy, pull your pull-ups down before you sit on the potty."

Nancy smiled at her mother, sat down on the potty chair with her pants on, then immediately stood up. "All done."

As Nancy walked out of the bathroom, an odor followed her.

"I believe our daughter needs a change. What an aroma! No more cabbage for our girl. George, I'm in the middle of cooking dinner. I know you changed her last but, do you mind?"

George changed Nancy's pull-up diaper. After she was cleaned, George took Nancy's hand in his and walked her over to her new potty chair. "Look! This is where the poopy goes—in the potty. Pee and poopy go in the potty. Okay?"

"I have a song for you, Nancy. It's the Potty Time song. Are you ready? Here it goes."

Potty time
It's potty time.
Yes, it's potty time.
Oh, it's potty potty potty time, very good time of day.
It's potty time.
Yes, it's potty time.
And when potty time comes, can poopy be far away?
Bring on the potty chair.
Turn on the lights.

> Bring out the potty book
> Bring on the wipes.
> 'Cause, it's potty potty potty time.
> Grace laughed. "Where did that one come from? Have you been watching Nancy's children's videos?"

If your child shows interest in the potty, try scheduling potty breaks throughout the day. Consider having both boys and girls sit down to urinate. After boys have mastered bowel training, urinating while standing will be easier. They probably won't have good aim when they're first learning to urinate.

Girls need to learn to wipe from front to back to prevent germs from getting into the vagina or bladder. Potty time is a good time to talk about names of body parts.

Some toilets have loud flushing sounds. The loud noise combined with the child's waste being sucked down may be frightening enough to cause disinterest in using the potty. After you dump the excretions in the toilet, flush together with his or her hand on top of yours. If the noise is too much for the kids, have them put their hands over their ears while you flush. After a few times they will expect the loud noise and not be bothered. Your calm will diminish any anxieties your child may have.

Many public bathrooms have an automatic flush that can scare children. Let the kids know ahead of time that the toilet has a "magic" flush and will flush all by itself. Sometimes the toilet flushes before the child is finished using it, making the child nervous. Just say, "What a silly magic flush. It didn't know you were finished." The kids might "scold" the flush because it wasn't "paying attention." Talking about what may happen ahead of time helps children know what to do in a new situation, and be less anxious.

Reinforcement for a potty job well done may be:

- Sticker chart; accumulated stickers may purchase video-time or something your child has a strong interest in
- Verbal praise
- Extra bedtime stories

Parenting... A Work in Progress

When your child completes a few weeks of successful potty use, it's time to allow him or her to pick out "big boy" or "big girl" underwear. Giving the child a choice of underwear may be the buy-in that makes for a positive potty training experience. Make sure clothing is easy to remove: no belts, overalls, or tights.

Expect accidents, and let your child know that he is not in trouble; accidents happen. When parents express displeasure about potty accidents, children may feel less willing to use the potty chair for fear of parental anger. Carry extra clothes in a plastic bag in the car. You never know when you will need them.

Often, children who have been potty trained for months will get so busy playing that they forget to stop until it is too late to make it to the bathroom. If the parent is positive, the child will model the parent's reaction. Reminders to use the bathroom first thing in the morning, before an outing, after meals, and before bedtime will lessen the occurrence of accidents. Make sure your child washes hands, using soap, after using the bathroom.

Nighttime bladder control takes longer than daytime. Use plastic coverings for the mattress and disposable training pants when your child sleeps. It may be several months before your child is nighttime trained. In rare cases it may take a few years.

Relax; have patience. Rushing potty training will only prolong time in diapers or pull-ups and create unnecessary stress on parents and children. Allotting enough time lets parents relax and enables successful potty training. A little bribery is not a terrible idea. I bribed with cookies. Small candies, cookies, or favorite treats in tiny amounts may increase potty use success. Children take great pride in successful potty use.

Cognitive Development in Infants and Toddlers

Toys and Play Materials

According to M. B. Bronson of the National Association for the Education of Young Children (NAEYC), the following toys and play materials support thinking ability in infants and toddlers.

From month two:

- Crib mobile
- Rattles and other sound-making toys on a handle
- Music boxes, MP3s, and CDs with gentle, regular rhythms, songs, and lullabies

Music can be calming, change the mood, and exercise both sides of the brain for ease of learning language and math development. Music with basic rhythms and varying tempos keeps children's interest. I danced with my children to all types of music.

From month six:

- Squeeze toys
- Nesting cups
- Clutch and texture balls
- Stuffed animals and soft-bodied dolls
- Filling and emptying toys
- Large and small blocks
- Pots, pans, and spoons from the kitchen
- Simple, floating objects for the bath
- Picture books

From year one:
- Large dolls
- Toy dishes
- Toy telephone
- Hammer-and-peg toy
- Pull and push toys
- Cars and trucks
- Rhythm instruments, such as bells, cymbals, and drums
- Simple puzzles
- Sandbox, shovel, and pail
- Shallow wading pool and water toys

Infants grasp the idea of physical reasoning early. Three- to four-month-olds realize solid objects collide. By five to six months of age, infants have learned by trial and error that a large object cannot go through a small opening (Sitskoorn & Smitsman, 1995).

Children six months and older get a big kick out of putting items in a container and taking them out. Bring out a plastic container with different sized baby safe items, like balls too big to fit in the mouth and let your child experiment with putting different sized items in the opening of the container.

I put child safety locks on all kitchen cabinets within my children's reach, but I kept one lower kitchen cabinet accessible to my children when they were old enough to crawl around and open cabinet doors. This cabinet contained plastic bowls and metal pans of varying size and large wooden spoons. Sometimes they made "music" by banging spoons on pans. Other times they wore plastic bowls for hats. Both daughters enjoyed splashing water in the bowls and pans. I kept big towels nearby if we did this activity indoors. Soaking up spilled water was part of water play, always carefully monitored.

Opportunities to explore the environment provide the enrichment necessary for strong cognitive growth. Each experience enhances the mind, making new connections within the brain. Walks to the park, visits to the museum, and playing with family and toys help children develop thinking skills. Speaking frequently to infants and toddlers, even during diaper changes, is particularly important for children's intelligence.

> Two-month-old Tina, wide awake in her bassinet, stared intently at the mobile above her. Tina's parents, Joe and Liz, folded clothing in the same room.
> Joe glanced at Tina. "Liz, look. I think Tina's trying to get at her mobile. Wait, she's kicking. Do you think she's getting the mobile to move on purpose? She's so young. My baby's a genius!"
> "It's possible Joe. Tina might have gotten smarter overnight."
> "She kicked again and the mobile moved. I really think she did that on purpose! Wait until I call my sister with the news. It's our bragging rights this time."

Infants as young as six months can imitate actions, such as pulling, pressing, and turning, they saw on an activity board the previous day (Collie & Hayne, 1999). By fourteen to fifteen months, toddlers can imitate the activities of peers and adults seen after a long delay, as much as several months later (Hannah & Meltzoff, 1993).

When speaking to an infant, many people instinctively use a form of speech with a higher pitch, melodious voice, and short sentences. This type of speech is called Parentese, or Motherese. This model of speech makes learning language easier for the baby. Take caution with the use of adult speech. Toddlers will remember what you say as well as what you do.

> Ramon and Victoria were new parents. Ramon had a rather colorful way of expressing himself. Neither parent realized how much of their language their daughter, Liana, was learning. She had recently turned two. Liana was one of those children who listened and waited to speak until she was ready.
> One afternoon, Ramon wrote a note and decided it wasn't needed. He crumpled the paper and tossed it at the trash can. It missed. Much to Ramon and Victoria's surprise, Liana said, "Say son of a bitch, Daddy. Say son of a bitch."

Parenting... A Work in Progress

> Victoria's chin dropped. She stared at her husband, "Good grief. That was her first sentence!"
>
> "Guess I need to tone down the language. I didn't know she heard me. Come to Daddy, Liana. Help me throw out the paper."

The best way to keep profanity out of children's language is for them never to hear it. In Liana's case, both of her parents need to alter their language usage and model polite verbiage. They need not be visibly upset when they hear their daughter use profanity—just correct her with calm voices. If a word is considered "naughty," a child will use it more often. Treating profane language as a minor issue at this young age should cause a lessening and then elimination of the "bad" words. If parents make bad language a huge issue, it will become a huge problem.

Self-Awareness

Around eighteen months of age, a toddler can look at her reflection in a mirror and realize she is looking at herself and not another child.

> Angela, nineteen months old, sat in front of a mirror. She saw a red spot on her nose. While applying makeup, mother had put some blush on Angela's nose earlier in the morning. Angela reached her hand toward her nose and touched it.
>
> Angela's mother picked up her daughter and gave her a big hug. "Look at you, my big girl. Do you want to get that red off? Let me help you."
>
> Angela grabbed the washcloth from her mother. "Down, mom-mom."
>
> "Okay, Angie, I'll put you down. Wipe your nose, then give Mommy the washcloth."
>
> Angela rubbed her nose with the cloth and kept it as she walked through the hallway to her parents' home office. Angela's father, sitting in front of his computer, turned to see Angela trip as she walked through the doorway.

> "Oops-a-daisy, Miss Maisy, there's my big girl. What do you have in your hand? Mommy, why does our girl have a red nose?"
>
> Angela's mother walked into the office and sat down on the sofa. "Angela helped me with my make-up this morning."

If Angela had been given the "red nose" test at a younger age, she would likely have pointed at the "baby" in the mirror or touched the mirror where she saw the red dot. In that case, Angela would be aware of the red dot but would think it is on the baby in the mirror, not herself. After seeing herself in the mirror, Angela grabbed her own nose, demonstrating that she is self-aware and understands she is the child in the mirror.

Angela's mother also asked her to do two things, one after the other. She was to wipe her nose and then give the washcloth back. At this age Angela is not being defiant when walking off with the washcloth. She only remembered one request.

Young children have short attention spans, a poor sense of time, and little self-control. Children improve in all these areas as the frontal lobe matures. This area of the brain is completely mature sometime in the mid-twenties.

The Red Nose Test

Apply a small amount of blush to the tip of the child's nose. Show the child her reflection. If the child reaches for the baby in the mirror, she is not yet self-aware. If she reaches for her own nose, the child is self-aware.

Self-Awareness and Language

Language and self-awareness go hand in hand. Part of the normal process of growing up is the struggle to be independent. Children and parents will not always share the same wishes and wants. The combination of self-awareness and the desire to be separate from parents' influence causes the proliferation of the word "No."

By the end of the second year, children achieve emotional self-awareness. They are aware of how they feel and have the language to express it. It is the beginning of becoming one's own person. This huge developmental step may be difficult for parents, as much effort has been expended to support and encourage their children. It is heartbreaking to feel them pull away, but it is necessary for children to grow into themselves.

Self-Regulation

Self-regulation is the ability to do what is necessary without outside influence. For example, I use self-regulation to fit into my favorite pair of pants by sticking to a diet and exercise plan. I find it difficult to say no to certain foods, so to help reach my goal, I tape a photo of myself wearing my favorite pants to the refrigerator. I have set my goal, am monitoring my behavior, and using willpower to achieve my goal of fitting into my favorite jeans.

Children develop the basic skills for self-regulation in the first five years of life (Blair, 2002; Galinsky, 2010). Parents can teach strategies to support their children's development of self-regulation by modeling appropriate behavior, using hints and cues, and gradually withdrawing parental support. When parents demonstrate appropriate behavior, they show their children how to accomplish a task and use the self-regulation needed to finish it. When parents use simple directions, gestures, and touch, they provide their children with valuable cues about how and when to regulate their emotions, attention, and behavior (Florez, 2011).

Parents can help children recognize and name their emotions by calmly saying to frustrated or angry babies and toddlers, "You sound angry," and then cuing them to start self-calming by using gentle touch and saying, "Relax," or "I'm here to help you." As children begin to use language, parents can provide hints about when and how to ask for help or when to try a different plan of action (Florez).

As children regularly direct their attention appropriately, persist in challenging tasks, and use their words to seek attention and help, they increase their ability to act independently. Parents may then give their children autonomy to regulate themselves, while checking their progress and stepping in when necessary to provide support (Florez).

Withdrawing parental support from infants, toddlers, and preschoolers requires constant monitoring by adults, as the younger the child, the more inconsistent self-regulation skills will be. Infants and toddlers who have learned to routinely self-calm need more support from parents when they are ill or in unfamiliar surroundings (Florez).

Young children who engage in intentional self-regulation learn more and go further in their education (Blair & Diamond 2008). The development of self-regulation in the areas of emotional and behavioral control is related to acceptance by peers, success in school, and the ability to more easily make life adjustments (Bronson, M. B., 2000).

Spontaneous Altruism

Soon after their first birthday, children begin to help other people spontaneously. Children as young as fourteen months have a natural tendency to assist other persons with their problems, even when the other is a stranger and they receive no reward. A reward for helping does not make the child inclined to help (Warneken & Tomasello, 2008). The reward can backfire, causing the child to be less willing to help. A thank you is enough.

Parents do not need to be present, requesting that the child help (Warneken & Tomasello, 2012). Even if a child is busy playing with a toy, he or she will stop playing in order to help. But when assistance from the child involves a sacrifice—giving up their own possession to lessen another's distress—the child has more difficulty helping (Grusec et al., 2002).

> Bob walked down the hallway, arms full of bags. His twenty-month-old son, Peter, watched as his father bumped into the door on the way to the kitchen to drop off groceries. The second time Peter saw his father walk to the door, Peter pushed the door open for his dad. Bob looked at his son and smiled. "Thanks, Peter. You're a big helper."

Parenting...A Work in Progress

> "I big," said Peter, still standing by the door.
> "All the groceries are in now, Petey. Go play."

Young children are ready to help selflessly, to comfort others, and help out with simple chores—unless their personal belongings are involved.

Language Development in Infants and Toddlers

Interpreting Baby Sounds

A father held his infant daughter, and when she pointed towards an object, he realized she wanted to know its name. The "finger of knowledge" was the precursor to the child asking, "Waz dat?" As an infant, she was unable to ask questions. Her use of body language indicated what she wanted to know.

Understanding language comes well before a child's ability to speak. During infancy the muscles within the child's mouth are not coordinated enough to make word sounds.

Various stages occur during the growth of language in typically developing children. Usually there are vowel sounds—cooing—followed later by sounds sometimes called "raspberries" that children do by sticking the tongue out and vibrating air over the lips.

Typical children are born able to hear all sounds of all languages on the planet. They imitate sounds they hear, losing the ability to mimic sounds they never hear. Look closely at a young child when he or she is exploring sounds. The mouth opens and closes. The tongue moves all around the mouth, exploring the possibilities.

If a child is exposed to more than one language, he will repeat what he hears with his best ability. Not all languages require the same placement of tongue, mouth, and facial muscles. Exercising different muscles allows the child to later achieve correct language accents.

According to Priscilla Dunstan, babies make universal sounds that have the same meaning. "Neh" means "I'm hungry." "Owh" means "I'm sleepy." "Heh" means "I'm uncomfortable, may need a change." "Eairh" means "I have tummy trouble." "Eh" means "I need to be burped."

Parenting... A Work in Progress

Dunstan, a mother and former opera singer, used her keen sense of sound recognition to pick out patterns in her son's cries. She noticed other babies made the same "words." If parents learn to recognize these sounds and attend to the babies' needs right away, all-out wails may be avoided (de la Torre, 3/15/2012). A study of Dunstan's method to be conducted with Brown University was cancelled, but the method works well for some. Interpreting cries takes practice.

Parents who observe their children's body language often have more content children. Children who are taught baby sign language can communicate their needs at an earlier age, which lessens their need to cry.

Soothe a Crying Infant

Babies will also cry when other babies do, a common occurrence in hospital nurseries.

The following methods may soothe a crying newborn:
- Hold the baby against the shoulder and rock back and forth or walk. Skin-to-skin or close contact is soothing for babies and allows them to be quietly alert.
- Massage the baby. Gentle massage relaxes the baby's muscles.
- Play soft sounds. Continuous sounds, like peaceful music, a ceiling fan, or a ticking clock effectively calm the baby.
- Make a shush sound into the baby's ear. This mimics the sound of the womb and calms the baby.
- Breathe deeply and relax.

Your calm will enhance the baby's calm. For toddlers, try distraction when they cry. One of my children was crying because she was hungry. She woke up ravenous. I gave her an empty box of oatmeal that had the Quaker Oats man on the front. The picture intrigued her long enough for me to get breakfast to the table without more tears.

If an infant doesn't seem alert to loud noises, check for hearing loss. Auditory Brainstem Response (ABR/BSER) is a test used as part of newborn screening. It estimates hearing sensitivity and identifies neurological abnormalities of the auditory nerve and the auditory pathway through the brain stem. If the baby can hear, brain wave activity in the "hearing" area of the brain will be measurable. If an infant fails the test, it is repeated because there may be fluid in the ears. If the baby still fails the test, the family will be referred to an audiologist who can perform the ABR and test for all decibels (Montoya, 2014).

Colic

Colic is uncontrollable crying in a healthy baby. The risk of colic is lowered if the baby is breastfed. Breast milk is easily digested, so there is less risk of digestive distress. A breastfed baby may still have symptoms of colic. It is possible that the baby may have an allergy or sensitivity to food the mother has eaten. If mother eats cabbage, baby will be gassy. Whatever mother eats and drinks becomes part of the makeup of the breast milk.

Prime allergy or sensitivity suspects are dairy, wheat, eggs, nuts, fruit, caffeine, and chocolate. If breastfeeding, try avoiding these foods for a few days. If the baby feels better, introduce the suspect foods back into the diet one at a time. If the baby is fussy after reintroducing a particular food, an offending food has been found. Inform your doctor if a particular food causes the baby to act fussy.

Colic might be caused by an imbalance of healthy bacteria in the intestines. Studies have shown that infants with colic have different intestinal bacteria than infants who don't suffer from colic. Treatment with probiotics (specifically *Lactobacillus reuteri*) has been shown to help some babies with colic symptoms. Ask your pediatrician for suggestions (reviewed by Palamountain, S. & Turner, T., 2013).

"Why Is My Baby Still Crying?"

Jacob, two months old, discovered that when he kicked the mattress of his bassinet with his heels, his mobile moved. That made him happy so he kicked again, causing the mobile to move again.

Later, when Jacob turned his head and looked towards the curtain across his bedroom, he kicked and the curtain moved. Jacob kicked again, but the

Parenting... A Work in Progress

> curtain did not move. This made Jacob angry, so he cried. Jacob's parents didn't know why he cried. Jacob didn't understand that the wind moved the curtain over his bedroom window. Thumping the mattress with his heels wouldn't make his curtain move.

Sometimes it is impossible to understand why a child cries. The parent is not at fault.

From Sounds to Words

As the muscles in and around the mouth develop and strengthen, interesting sounds emanate from children. At two months, infants can produce vowel sounds: cooing. By four months, infants add consonant sounds: babbling. Around twelve months, babies begin to make first words.

The first word is often the name of a person close to the child — most often but not always Ma or Da, if the language the child hears is English.

> The first time Mrs. Eliott heard the "ma" sound, she was excited. At the time she believed her daughter, Sarah, was calling her name. In truth, it is more likely Mrs. Eliott happened to hear the sound ma and positively reinforced the repetition of the sound by using a happy voice. "You said Mama! Say Mama, ma ma ma." Mother and child played the word game, and eventually Sarah attached that particular sound to the person who cared for her daily: Mom.

The word Ma or Mama was meaningful for both mother and child and further cemented the parent–child bond and child–parent attachment.

At approximately eighteen months, toddlers form meaningful two-word combinations. "Daddy go" may mean Daddy is going to work. "Tommy car" may mean the toy car belongs to Tommy. Two-word utterances have a lot of meaning.

Infants and Toddlers—Ages Birth through Two Years

By two years of age, children begin to increase the length of sentences.

> My oldest child, Laurel, had an interesting first phrase. She said, "Mom, stone in nose." It was not exactly what I expected for a first phrase, but it was extremely informative. I looked, and there it was. A turquoise colored stone that looked like it might have come from the bottom of a fish tank. Good grief, this wasn't in any parenting manual!
>
> My first thought was to get the stone out. I knew if I tried to poke at it, the stone would just slip further up her nostril. Handing my daughter a tissue, I said, "Laurel, blow your nose."
>
> She sniffed it all the way in.
>
> Off we went to the doctor's office. The stone was too far up Laurel's nose to remove in the office, so we drove her to the hospital.
>
> I brought Laurel's favorite toy, a baby doll, with her to the hospital. The wonderful staff allowed Laurel to keep the doll with her, adorned with a blue hair net just like the one she had to wear. Later, the doctor came out to say that Laurel was doing well. The surgery took longer than expected because the stone kept slipping farther up the sinus passage. The doctor told me that it was a surprisingly sterile stone.
>
> My daughter Julia's first phrase was also quite informative, but not as traumatic. "Mom, tummy hurt." After that, she proceeded to vomit all over me and the bathroom floor. This happened right after Easter. Julia had located the Easter candy and enjoyed munching it down, much to the dismay of her digestive system. Candy would later be stored well out of reach.

During the span of two short years, a child begins with crying and moving his or her mouth indiscriminately to speaking in meaningful phrases—a huge developmental leap. Children exposed to a lot of language will have an expanded vocabulary. They will use the vocabulary of their parents and other caregivers. The use of Parentese, with higher pitched voice, short sentences, and melodious tone, makes learning language easier for children.

Second Language Learning

The critical age for children to learn language is between birth and age twelve. A second language may be taught to children starting around age two while they can still hear different phonetic pronunciations. It is easier to speak the second language with the accent of a native speaker when learning the second language as a young child. Younger is better, but it is still possible to become fully bilingual as an adult (Singleton, & Lengyel, 1995).

In bilingual people, the earlier in life the second language is learned, the more similar the areas of the brain involved in understanding and producing the two languages. Brain-imaging studies have shown when people learn a second language later in life, the areas of the cortex involved in understanding the two languages are not always the same. When bilingual people lose the use of one of their languages as the result of a brain injury, the language that they retain is not always necessarily their mother tongue (thebrain.mcgill.ca).

The tiny country of Luxembourg, bordering Belgium, France, and Germany, has three official languages: French, German, and Luxembourgish. At a typical school in Luxembourg, children learn to be literate in German, French, and Luxembourgish languages. They learn to read and write in German from the first year in primary school. In their second year, they learn French and then Luxembourgish grammar. By the age of eight, children have learned three languages. In secondary school, they learn English and a second language of choice (expatica.com). People native to Luxembourg often speak five languages.

People fluent in more than one language tend to be flexible, creative thinkers.

Temperament, Bonding and Attachment in Infants and Toddlers

Temperament

A child's temperament is her personal "style"—how she interacts with the world. Understanding a child's temperament can help parents:
- relate and react to her world;
- perceive the child's strengths;
- understand what support the child may need to be successful in life.

Temperaments may be divided into three types:
- Easy (40 percent of children): They are often happy and have a regular routine of eating and sleeping; they are adaptable and easy to soothe.
- Difficult (10 percent of children): These children are often cranky and have an irregular routine of eating and sleeping; they are easily upset and have difficulty adjusting to new experiences.
- Slow-to-warm-up (15 percent of children): They are cautious and negative in mood; they adjust slowly to new experiences.

Not all children fit neatly into these three categories. About thirty-five percent of children show blends of temperamental characteristics (Berk, 2002).

The greatest difficulties arise when parents and children have different temperaments. A slow-to-warm-up parent may have trouble understanding why her son is uninhibited. A parent with an easy temperament will have difficulty understanding why his daughter is often cranky.

> Jennifer's family was large and boisterous. Life in her family was full of activity. The arrival of another baby brought happiness to their home. This was to be the last child adopted into their household. Baby Joy was not a happy girl. She slept poorly and was easily upset. Loud noise startled her and made her cry. Jennifer, the oldest child in the family at 16, was seriously worried about her newest sibling.
>
> Jennifer sat next to her mother, who tried to soothe the baby. "Mom, what's wrong with Joy? Everybody cries when they're babies, but this is ridiculous."
>
> "I was worried about that, too. Your dad and I went to the doctor's office to see if Joy was ill. There is nothing physically wrong with her. The doctor believes it just may be the way she is."
>
> "You're kidding, right? Did Dr. Kiltner have any suggestions?"
>
> "She says sometimes there are personality differences. Evidently, Joy is having a hard time adjusting to the noise and activity we normally have around here. Her suggestion is to try and lower the sound level and let Joy slowly adjust to life with us."
>
> "Sounds like time for a family meeting, huh, Mom?"

Temperament has a genetic component. Both parents may be easygoing, but the child might have inherited an uncle's foul temper. That may be modified.

A young child may be shy and take time to warm up to people, while in eighth grade, this same child may begin to assert herself, joining team activities in school. Her shy, slow-to-warm-up temperament adapted to her day-to-day experiences. Parents cannot force a change in temperament, but they can alter the extremes by changing the environment and offering the child new experiences.

Bonding

Bonding is the relationship of the parent or other caregiver to the child that may begin as early as the confirmation of conception. This feeling of affection and concern for the new baby can bring out a macho man's inner marshmallow. Some parents develop strong affection when first holding their newborn. For others, the emotion develops gradually (Lamb, 1994).

There is a two-year "window of opportunity" to develop this bonding relationship. The strength of the parent–child or other caregiver–child bond helps ensure the child will not be harmed or abandoned during the difficult developmental periods, such as the terrible twos and adolescence (Toma, 2014). The caregiver bonding relationship sets the stage for the attachment relationship of the child to the parents. Bonding and attachment are distinctly separate yet interweave to begin the building of the parent/caregiver–child relationship.

Attachment

According to John Bowlby (1969/1982, 1973), the attachment relationship serves to reduces stress and regulate emotions, thereby promoting the child's willingness to explore the environment. Bowlby believed infants whose mothers responded appropriately and quickly to their cues, such as soothing a crying infant, learn that they can count on Mom when they need help.

Attachment is the child's tie to his parents or caregivers. Attachment, which begins at birth, is related to an understanding that people continue to exist even when they cannot be seen. Attachment may be measured using the "Strange Situation" test when the child is eighteen months old.

The Strange Situation test, developed by psychologist Mary Ainsworth, is a method to determine a child's attachment style. The child and parent (typically mother) are put in a room with toys and other interesting items. Mother lets the child explore the room by herself. After exploration time, a stranger enters the room and speaks to the mother. The stranger approaches the child and mother leaves the room. Soon afterward the mother returns, comforts her child, and leaves again. This time the stranger leaves too. After a few minutes the stranger returns and interacts with the child. Then mother returns to greet her child.

The child's reactions determine which of four attachment styles—secure, avoidant, resistant, or disorganized—the child exhibits.

Two signs that the attachment between parent and child is secure are:

- Baby is confident of parent's support;
- Baby uses parent as a secure base from which to explore the environment (Bowlby, 1988).

> Eighteen month old Alice walked across the kitchen floor, past her mother, and into the living room. Two minutes later, Alice walked back to the doorway between the two rooms. Seeing her mother was still in the kitchen, Alice returned to the living room, grabbed her stuffed dog, Clifford, and gave it a big squeeze.
>
> Alice dropped Clifford as soon as she heard her mother talking on the phone. She walked back into the kitchen and saw her mother sitting on a chair. Alice pulled on the leg of her mother's pants.
>
> "Just a minute, Zoey. Alice, it's your Auntie Zoey on the phone. Do you want to say hi?"
>
> Alice's mother scooped up her daughter who immediately grabbed the phone and put it against her ear. Alice, hearing her aunt's voice, turned the phone around and stared at it.
>
> "Give it back to Mommy, Alice. Look, Alice, here's a spoon." Alice let go of the phone and took the long-handled, wooden spoon and squirmed. Her mother let Alice off of her lap. She wanted to wander through the house.
>
> "Sorry, Zoey, Alice isn't ready for the phone yet. She is so cute; just stops by to check on me every few minutes."

Alice uses her mother as a secure base from which to explore her world, which for now is the house. A secure attachment enables confidence. Children with secure attachments are more likely to feel comfortable exploring the environment, leading to greater intelligence.

There are three types of insecure attachments:

- **Avoidant.** Babies are unresponsive to parents, are not distressed when they leave, and when picked up do not always cling. These children shut down and give the appearance of not needing a parent. (Caused by parents who are distant and unresponsive and linked to later lack of empathy in child.)
- **Resistant.** Infants are clingy when the parent is there, angry when the parent returns, and are not easily comforted. These children are reluctant to leave the parents to explore for fear that no one will be there to help. (Caused by erratic, unpredictable care of children.)
- **Disorganized/disoriented.** Infants appear dazed and confused, sometimes showing a flat, depressed look. These children do not seem to know how to approach their parents for comfort or attention. (Caused by parents exhibiting threatening behavior toward the child.)

Children exhibiting insecure attachments may be helped by interventions that teach their parents to follow the child's lead (Cohen et al., 1999) or by watching their child using video feedback (Juffer et al., 2004) to focus the parents' attention on the child's behavior (Berlin et al., 2005).

Some parents had poor attachments with their own parents. Denying the pains of childhood only increases the risk that it will continue to the next generation. Consider the following:

- Face what was hurtful.
- Know that the memories may still be of influence.
- Think about the positive memories you want to pass on.
- Find as many positive parenting resources as possible.

Many adults had difficult childhoods and feel poorly attached to their parents. We cannot go back and change what has been done. We can

Parenting... A Work in Progress

make a conscious decision to do better with our own children. Whenever I felt myself turning into my own parents, I stopped, physically took a step back, and remembered I am me. I know a better way.

Quickly, think of something positive. Enjoyable thoughts bring relaxation. A calmer emotional state helps un-cloud the mind, freeing it from anger—an emotion based in fear.

In terms of attachment, it does not matter whether Mom, Dad, or both work outside the home. Daycare does not detract from parent–child attachment. If parents are responsive and sensitive to their children's cues, the attachment will be secure.

An important consideration is to keep the daycare provider consistent so children can form an attachment to the daycare provider, too.

Emotional and Social Development in Infancy and Toddlerhood

Emotional Expression

Happiness is contagious. When an infant smiles, the parent is encouraged to be affectionate and smile in return, so the baby smiles more. In early infancy, newborns smile during sleep, while being rocked, and in response to soft sounds and touch. By one month, infants smile at eye-catching, interesting sights. The social smile begins during the second month (Sroufe & Waters, 1976).

> Kathy and Bob brought their first baby, Aaron, home from the hospital. Bob appeared to handle being a dad with ease. Kathy wondered how on earth she was ever going to be able to be a parent. All Aaron seemed to do was cry, eat, and poop. He did not sleep anywhere near enough. Karen's friends suggested she sleep when the baby slept, but the house was a disaster zone. The clutter drove her crazy, although it might have been sleep deprivation that threatened to tip her over the ragged edge.
> In frustration, Karen sobbed on the phone. "I'm not cut out for this. What was I thinking? I don't think I like my baby. What's wrong with me? Don't all parents love their child right away?"
> Two states away, Karen's mother wished she could transport herself directly to her daughter. Karen was in desperate need of a hug and help. "Karen, can't Bob

take time off work? I think one of the reasons you're so upset is lack of sleep."

"Bob did get family leave, but it was only for one week. He had to go back. I wish you didn't live so far away. Are you still coming to stay with us for a while?"

"Of course. I'm set to fly in on Saturday morning. Don't worry about anything. Bob doesn't need to pick me up. I'll get a rental car and drive myself. I love you, Karen. Now, promise me you'll get a nap in."

"Okay, I promise. I love you, Mom."

Karen's mother helped cook, clean, and took turns holding her grandbaby. The presence of more loved ones helped Karen get through some of the depression she felt. Extra sleep made an enormous difference.

Aaron still breastfed every few hours, but Karen felt more confident and better about being a mother. Holding and rocking her son, Karen looked down at his tiny fingers and sleepy face. Aaron opened his eyes, gazed at his mother, and smiled. Karen felt her heart warm towards her baby boy. She smiled back at Aaron. "Hello, my handsome little man."

Aaron smiled at his mother, eyes wide and sparkling.

"You are my boy! I needed that smile. Now I feel like you're mine. I love you, Aaron."

Laughter occurs around three to four months, usually during play with a caregiver. "Peek-a-boo" or "I'm gonna get you" may elicit baby giggles. Laughing at something external is an early sign of intelligence. Around six months, infants laugh and smile more frequently with familiar people, strengthening the parent–child bond.

At four months, when laughter has begun, angry responses increase. As infants become capable of acting on the immediate environment, they want to control their actions. If a desired toy is removed, or the infant does not want to be put down for a nap, the baby's body tenses and loud angry crying begins.

As early as three months, babies express sadness when interaction with a parent is disrupted. When parents or other caregivers ignore the infant's attempts to get adults to respond, the baby turns away and cries.

Stranger Anxiety

A wariness of unfamiliar adults is called stranger anxiety. This fear of the unknown occurs about the same time babies begin to crawl. This keeps the young child close to parents and careful about unfamiliar people and objects. Stranger anxiety begins when children remember objects and specific people that are not present, around the second half of the first year.

Not all infants and toddlers are wary of strangers. Temperament, which is inherited, and experience with other people affect the child's level of anxiety. An infant accustomed to being handled by many people shows little stranger anxiety.

> Sarah and Marnie, both eight months old, lived in the same apartment complex. Sarah attended daycare full time at her father's place of work. Marnie stayed at home with her mother, June.
>
> Sarah's mother, Graciela, saw June in the courtyard of their building, walking her daughter in a stroller. "June! How are you holding up? I haven't seen you in a while. How is your adorable Marnie?"
>
> Graciela peeked into June's stroller to say hello to her. Marnie scrunched her nose and let out a wailing cry. "Well, where did that come from? Marnie, you know who I am."
>
> "Marnie does this all the time now. I don't understand it. Just a second. Shh Marnie, it's our friend, Graciela. Don't cry. Here, take your binky."
>
> Marnie sucked on her pacifier while she stared at Graciela from the safety of her stroller.
>
> "This all started last week totally out of the blue. My mother-in-law sat down next to me while I was

> holding Marnie, held out her arms to give her a hug, and Marnie whipped her head around and didn't want anything to do with her grandmother. Nana seemed so sad. I feel awful about it."
>
> "What about you? Does Sarah act this shy when she's around other people?"
>
> "Actually, Sarah doesn't seem to mind being around others. She sees so many different people during the week, I guess it doesn't bother her.

Between seven and ten months, infants can respond to others' emotions. Babies begin to look to parents' reactions to know how to react in a new situation. This social referencing, common in toddlerhood, helps the child avoid harmful situations (Meltzoff, 1988). It is also a way to unintentionally transmit the fears and anxieties of the parent to the child.

> Carla was terrified of spiders. When she was six years old, her older brothers left a tarantula on her bed. They laughed at her when she screamed for help. The boys were punished by their parents for teasing and being mean to their little sister. Every night for at least a month Carla checked all around her room, especially underneath the bed, for unwanted arachnids.
>
> As an adult with small children, Carla remained fearful of spiders. Not wanting to transmit her fear to her children, she researched different types of spiders in the area near their home. Fortunately no black widow or brown recluse spiders frequented their neighborhood. While looking up tarantulas, Carla discovered that although they are large and hairy, no one has ever died of a tarantula bite. Indiana Jones was never in any danger from the many tarantulas on his back. "No wonder the boys had no trouble picking up that big old spider and putting it on my bed. There was nothing to be afraid of! Arrgg . . . brothers!"

> The local pet store had tarantulas in glass aquariums. Carla took her children to the pet store. Kyle, the oldest, helped his mom push his little sister, Kate, in a stroller. Look over here. See the Chilean rose tarantula? Isn't it beautiful? It can live as long as twenty years and likes to eat bugs."
> "Really? Cool mom! Hey, look, it's lifting up its front legs. I think it's mad."
> "I think you're right. Let's leave the spider alone and go check out the fish."
> Carla and her children left the pet store with a new fishbowl, fish food, and two green tetra fish. Carla's hands were sweaty from when she stood in front of the tarantula's aquarium, but having glass between the spider and herself, plus the need to put on a brave face for her children, let Carla release some of her anxiety while not transmitting a fear of spiders to her kids.

Social Referencing

Young children have a large impact on those around them. When they smile, parents smile in return. The same goes for laughter and unhappiness. Children look to parents to know how to react to new experiences.

When a parent panics, the child feels the parent's fear, and that fear may be transmitted to the child. Many fears are learned. Carla was able to calmly face her fear, so her children did not pick up her phobia of spiders. She approached the tarantula as she would any other creature in the pet store, so her son, who was tall enough to get a close look at the tarantula, saw it as one of the cool pets in the store.

Sleep and Sleep Disorders in Infants and in New Parents

Newborns sleep anywhere between sixteen and twenty hours per day and stay awake between one to two hours at a time. Infants sleep a total of thirteen to fifteen hours including naps. Toddlers sleep about twelve hours, including an afternoon nap.

The REM or rapid eye movement state in adults and children is the dream state. According to Dr. Allen Greene, dreaming begins two or three months before birth. Young infants spend about half of their sleep in REM. Their eyes move beneath the lids, slight body movements occur, and heart rate, blood pressure, breathing are uneven. During NREM or non-rapid eye movement sleep, body activity is minimal, and heart beat and breathing are regular. The rapid movement of the eyes during REM sleep helps supply oxygen to the eyes.

Given that the visual part of the brain is more active during newborn REM sleep than adult REM sleep, infants probably have more vivid visual dreams (Greene, 1999). Since infants and toddlers lack the ability to communicate their experiences, no one knows with surety what they dream about.

An irregular sleep pattern indicates possible abnormalities in the central nervous system, which suggests difficulties learning while awake (Halpern et al., 1995).

Sleep-Deprived Parents

It is possible to live a long time without enough sleep, but no one performs well without enough rest. In extreme cases, hallucinations may occur due to sleep deprivation.

Infants and Toddlers—Ages Birth through Two Years

Candice knew she should sleep while her baby, Cameron, slept, but the clutter in the house drove her to distraction. She didn't ask for help, feeling she could do it all herself.

One night Candice heard Cameron cry and sat up in bed, looking for her child. She saw her baby on top of the bed, under the family cat. Distraught with the cat, she picked it up by the scruff of its neck and threw it off the bed. The cat landed feet first and ran out of the bedroom. Candice gently scooped up her baby—or tried to. There was no Cameron. She gathered air in her arms. Panicked, she tried to pick up her child once more. Still no baby.

Remembering that she placed Cameron in her bassinet before falling asleep, Candice stumbled out of bed to check on her child. Cameron slept. Her tiny tummy rose up and down in an even rhythm.

"Oh, no! What's wrong with me?" Candice whispered.

In the morning Candice related the evening's event to her husband.

"Candice, how much sleep are you actually getting?"

"I don't know, Karl. I sleep when I can."

"If you're hallucinating, you're seriously not getting enough rest. Let me get a pad of paper. We'll write down what happens in a typical day. There has to be some time during the day for you to sleep."

Candice got up.

"No! Let me get it. Please, stay there, and I'll be right back." Karl turned back and smiled at Candice. "You don't have to wait on me. I love you."

Karl and Candice determined that she was sleeping five hours a day, all of it interrupted by either Cameron's needs or Candice's feelings of guilt for not being able to do everything herself.

> "Candice, I know you're used to having the household in a certain order, but you have to take care of yourself. How can you function at your best if you don't take care of you? I can help more with the house, and if you can deal with frozen dinners, I'll help cook."
>
> Candice nuzzled her head into Karl's shoulder. "It would mean a lot to me if you'd help tidy up a bit and help with dinner. I'm good with frozen dinners. You're mom says you were born to defrost!"
>
> "I see your sense of humor is still intact."

Postpartum Depression

Candice suffered from postpartum blues, "the baby blues," and felt overwhelmed with mood swings, occasional crying spells, and trouble sleeping. She worried she might develop severe postpartum depression, like her best friend, Fiona, who became suicidal within one month after delivering her baby. Fortunately, most of Candice's symptoms ended about two weeks after Cameron came home from the birthing center. As soon as she got more sleep, she completely recovered from the blues.

Some possible symptoms of postpartum depression include the following:

- Obsessive–compulsive thought and behavior.
- Feeling emotionally numb.
- Extreme mood swings.
- Loss of interest in regular activities.
- Appetite change.
- Feeling unable to love the baby or family.
- Too much or too little sleep.
- Inability to sleep.
- Extreme concern or lack of interest in the baby.
- Panic attacks.
- Anger towards baby or family members.
- Fear of harming baby or self.

Thoughts and/or attempts of suicide (the intent or attempt to kill oneself) and homicide (the intent or attempt to kill another person) exhibit real risks of postpartum depression (WebMD).

Children change everything: adult time, spare time, sleep, food. Exercise—who has time or energy for that? Parents-to-be, knowledgeable about the growth and development of their fetus, discover they are months behind the learning curve after their child is born. The baby is up to speed, and the poor parents have to play catch-up.

The baby has many needs. Sleepless nights, financial demands, and little to no adult time stress the relationship between mother and father. Consider the following ideas to help ease the transition to parenthood:

- Make a plan to share household chores. Decide on chores by skill and time, not gender. Reevaluate as needed.
- Share child care as soon as the baby comes home. Discuss parenting concerns often.
- Communicate concerns about decisions and responsibilities. Listen to your partner's point of view. Be willing to compromise.
- Balance parenting and work. Try to cut back extra work hours if it is too much.
- Be proactive with lawmakers regarding family needs. On-site, affordable daycare, flexible work hours, and paid leave go a long way towards helping parents with young children.

Of all the suggestions for transitioning to parenthood, communication between parents is of utmost importance. Lack of communication is the beginning of the end in any relationship.

Newborn babies sleep much of the day; however, that sleep is not grouped in long time allotments. This interrupted pattern of sleep is hard on the adult body, which generally needs an average of seven or eight hours of rest. Lack of sleep may lead to poor coordination, faulty judgment, and, in worst cases, hallucinations. Parents must keep lines of communication open to share the events of their days. Communication calls for listening, not merely hearing. Be willing to compromise about chores and other responsibilities. Ask for help if it is needed.

SIDS - Sudden Infant Death Syndrome

Sudden Infant Death Syndrome (SIDS) is the unexpected death of an infant under one year of age, usually at night, that remains unexplained. One theory suggests that, when breathing temporarily stops in sleep, the baby's brain does not tell the respiratory system to inhale, causing death by asphyxiation. Smoking during and after pregnancy, prenatal depressant drug usage, infants sleeping on their stomachs, and excessive body warmth put a strain on the respiratory control area of the baby's brain. The strain may cause the respiratory control center to stop working.

Researchers at the University of Adelaide's School of Medical Sciences found that SIDS may be related to an inherited sleep apnea problem. They found remarkable similarities between the brains of babies who died of SIDS and children who died of accidental asphyxiation (Lund Jensen et al., 2014).

Surviving family members may need help overcoming their grief. Support groups of parents who have experienced the same tragedy help each other cope. The CJ Foundation (www.cjsids.org) has a free online parent-to-parent support group for people who have suffered the sudden or unexpected loss of an infant. It is moderated by a social worker (click "Grief and Bereavement" to learn more about the online support group). SIDS America has a faith-based website (www.sidsamerica.org/sids-help/sids-support-groups) which families may find helpful. These are two of many sites found during a web search. Health care providers, friends, family, neighbors, workplace, and faith communities are all available to help.

Studies have suggested that co-sleeping during the newborn's first few months increases the number of brief, spontaneous arousals from sleep, which may decrease SIDS (McKenna et al., 1990; McKenna et al., 1993; Mosko et al., 1997).

Prenatal Drug Use

Lilly tried to ignore her pregnancy. She consumed drugs to remove herself from the realities of her existence. She preferred to float on the island of "zoning out" instead of facing the restricted life she made for herself. After burning the bridges of family and friends, she avoided human contact for the cravings of heroin and her main drug of choice, methamphetamine.

Fear permeated her thoughts as the smoke from her cigarette filled her lungs. Lilly knew she needed help. She couldn't rid herself of her addictions by herself. She remembered Madeleine, a friend from childhood with whom she still maintained contact. In a panic, Lilly called her friend, confessed her addiction, and begged for help. She told Madeleine she'd decided to clear the drugs out of her system. Lilly didn't want to harm her baby.

Madeleine and her mother worried for Lilly and her developing child. They offered to help in any way they were able. Although they offered to share their home, Lilly opted to remain in her current apartment. For several months Lilly made progress. She improved her nutritional habits and made some appointments with the doctor to monitor her pregnancy.

The siren's call for drugs proved too strong. Lilly disappeared.

Late one afternoon, Lilly called Madeleine from the hospital. She was in labor. She had no one else to call. Madeleine and her mother arrived at the hospital within the hour. They coached Lilly through the delivery of a full-term beautiful baby boy. Lilly named him William.

The nurse in the delivery room asked if Lilly would be breastfeeding her son. She said no due to her past drug usage. Lilly's and William's blood were tested. Both had drugs in their systems. The Department of Child Services was called immediately after both heroin and methamphetamine were found in William's blood. Beautiful William entered life in withdrawal.

After almost two weeks in neonatal intensive care withdrawing from drugs, Lilly took William home. Child Protective Services monitored Lilly and she joined a program that enabled visitors to stop by to help her and her newborn baby. Madeleine was a member of the program.

Soon after coming home from the hospital, Lilly relapsed and returned to drug use.

Madeleine stopped by one evening to see how Lilly and baby William were faring. William was listless and glassy-eyed. When asked when she last fed the baby, Lilly could not remember. Looking around the kitchen, Madeleine noticed the cans of baby formula she had dropped off a few days earlier were still in the same spot she'd left them. Madeleine feared for William's life. She didn't know how to talk to Lilly without making her angry, so she called her mother, Georgia, for help.

Georgia reacted quickly. After some discussion, Lilly agreed to let William go home with Madeleine and Georgia. William was less than a month old.

Georgia asked for and was granted guardianship. William now had three moms: Lilly, Georgia, and Madeleine.

Lilly went to rehab in an attempt to break her drug habit. After rehab, she disappeared for three months. Lilly's decision to treat her body as she did affected everyone her son encountered.

Infants and Toddlers—Ages Birth through Two Years

During the next three years, Lilly spent less and less time with William. She missed his third birthday and third Christmas.

From infancy, William cried frequently. By the time he turned one, he would stand up and shake with rage. He was removed from several daycare situations due to pinching, biting, and head-banging himself and the other children. Several times William banged his head with such force he knocked himself out for a few seconds, terrifying caregivers. Just before William's second birthday, he was diagnosed with nervous ticks. He also had an increasing number of allergies. William, hyperactive, was diagnosed with developmental delays and sensory issues.

William often spaced out, eyes glassy and vacant. No one knew where he went inside his head. To bring him back, Madeleine would hold his arm and call his name. Awareness would shine in his eyes and he would return as if nothing ever happened.

Now three years old, William attends preschool. Georgia and Madeleine consider developmental preschool part of the family support system. Positive social behavior is reinforced in school. William learns that he is not the only one who gets in trouble. At home, Madeleine discovered that using eye contact and the following sentences can shorten a temper-tantrum: "You need to listen with your ears. I'm talking to you." William responds positively to Madeleine's combination of eye contact and simple statements. She has requested his teachers use the same method to keep behaviors from escalating. This action reinforces home-school cohesion. William sees and hears similar discipline techniques in the important places of his young life.

Georgia and Madeleine frequently feel overwhelmed. William's food allergies intensify as he ages.

> He has become food phobic—frightened to try any new foods. When visiting a restaurant, Madeleine enters first and wipes down the table and chairs before William sits down in an effort to avoid any allergic reactions. A pleasant day trip to the zoo is often a wakeful nightmare. Extra care must be taken. Food allergens are everywhere.
>
> Madeleine provides much of the day-to-day care for William. She researches methods to help him. She worries about his violent temper, wondering how he will cope with life as he ages.
>
> "Mr. Blankie" helps him deal with some of his sensory issues. He has learned to hold his blanket closely around his body and stroke the silky edge to calm himself. Madeleine knows William will eventually have to transition to another object of comfort. The blanket cannot go everywhere with him, especially as he becomes a bigger boy.
>
> The preschool provided a method William may use to calm himself. He raises his right index finger and says to himself, "Smell the flower." Then he inhales and exhales on the same finger, and says, "Blow out the candle." By repeating this method several times, William relaxes.

Some of the effects of methamphetamine exposure *in utero* include extreme irritability, behavioral disorders, learning deficits (particularly in the area of language), and extreme sensory sensitivity. Effects of heroin exposure *in utero* include high-pitched cries shortly after birth, irritability, interrupted sleep patterns, and poor tolerance to environmental changes (Nelson & Schohl, 2010).

Children whose mothers smoked during pregnancy are more likely to have behavioral problems, as well as allergies and asthma (Woolston; Wakschlag et al., 2002). William experienced most of these symptoms. Many of his complications may be lessened with positive parenting, school, and community assistance, particularly in the areas of physical and mental health.

> Madeleine was asked what she has found to enjoy about William. "He is really funny! When he learns something, he acts it out. One day I was talking to him at home, and he stopped me and said, "Mom, you have to raise your hand before you talk." I told him he was not the boss. Then he said, "Bikma's (his teacher's name) the boss." I knew then that he was actually learning in school."

Lilly's decision to treat her body as she did affected many more than herself and her son. Everyone William encounters is affected. The combination of toxic substances—tobacco, heroin, and methamphetamines—and early neglect caused a physical and psychological rip in his life's fabric that manifests through the lives of all those he touches.

References for Infants and Toddlers

National Safety Council (2009). Baby-proofing your home. Retrieved from http://www.nsc.org/news_resources.

Berk, L. (2002). *Infants, children, and adolescents* (pp. 155-263). Boston, MA: Allyn & Bacon.

Blair, C. (2002). School readiness: Integrating cognition and emotion in a neurobiological conceptualization of children's functioning at school entry. *American Psychologist, 57,* 111–27.

Blair, C., & Diamond, A. (2008). Biological processes in prevention and intervention: The promotion of self-regulation as a means of preventing school failure. *Development and Psychopathology, 20,* 899–911.

Bowlby, J. (1988). *A Secure Base.* New York, NY: Basic Books.

Bray, F., McCarron, P., & Parkin, D. M. (8/26/2004). The changing global patterns of female breast cancer incidence and mortality. *Breast Cancer Research, 6,* 229-239. Also may be retrieved from http://breast-cancer-research.com/content/6/6/229.

Bowlby, J. (1982). *Attachment. Attachment and loss* (2nd ed., Vol. 1). New York, NY: Basic Books. (Original work published in 1969.)

Bowlby, J. (1973). *Separation: Anxiety and anger. Attachment and loss* (Vol. 2). New York, NY: Basic Books.

Bronson, M. B. (2000). *Self-regulation in early childhood: Nature and nurture.* New York, NY: Guilford Press.

Bronson, M. B. (1995). *The right stuff for children birth to 8.* Washington, D.C.: National Association for the Education of Young Children.

CJ Foundation for SIDS (2014). Unexplained infant deaths. Retrieved from http://www.cjsids.org.

Cohen, N. J., Muir, E., Parker, C. J., Brown, M., Lojkasek, M., Muir, R., & Barwick, M. (1999). Watch, wait, and wonder: Testing the effectiveness of a new approach to mother-infant psychotherapy. *Infant Mental Health Journal, 20,* 429-451.

Colic: What is it? (2013) (reviewed by Palamountain, S., & Turner, T., pediatricians at Texas Children's Hospital in Houston, TX).

Retrieved from http://www.babycenter.com/0_colic-what-is-it_77.bc.

Collie, R., & Hayne, H. (1999). Deferred imitation by 6- and 9-month-old infants: More evidence for declarative memory. *Developmental Psychology, 35,* 83-90.

Cincinnati Children's Hospital Medical Center (2012). Craniosynostosis. Retrieved from http://www.cincinnatichildrens.org/health/c/craniosynostosis/.

de la Torre, N. (3/15/2012). Cracking the code: The secret language of babies. *SheKnows.* Retrieved from http://www.sheknows.com/parenting/articles/952759/cracking-the-code-the-secret-language-of-babies.

Eliot, L. (1999). What's going on in there? How the brain and mind develop in the first five years of life. New York, NY: Bantam.

Fagard, J., & Pezé, A. (1997). Age changes in interlimb coupling and the development of bimanual coordination. *Journal of Motor Behavior, 29,* 199-208.

Field, T. M., Schanberg, S. M., Scafidi, F., Bauer, C. R., Vega-Lahr, N., Garcia, R., Nystrum, J., & Kuhn, C. M. (1986). Effects of tactile/kinesthetic stimulation on preterm neonates. *Pediatrics, 77,* 654-658.

Florez, I. R. (07/2011). Developing young children's self-regulation through everyday experiences. *Young Children, 66*(4). Washington, DC: National Association for the Education of Young Children.

Galinsky, E. (2010). *Mind in the making: The seven essential life skills every child needs.* National Association for the Education of Young Children, special edition. New York, NY: HarperCollins.

Greer, F.R., Sicherer, S.H., Burks, W.A., & the Committee on Nutrition and Section on Allergy and Immunology (2008). Effects of early nutritional interventions on the development of atopic disease in infants and children: The role of maternal dietary restriction, breastfeeding, timing of introduction of complementary foods, and hydrolyzed formulas. *Pediatrics, 121*(1), 183-91. See

more at: http://www.kidswithfoodallergies.org/resourcespre.
php?id=108#sthash.G6T5dwsx.dpuf.

Greene, A. (7/23/1999). The Truth about Dreams, Nightmares and Night Terrors. Retrieved from http://www.drgreene.com/qa-articles/truth-dreams-nightmares-night-terrors.

Grusec, J. E., Davidov, M., & Lundell, L. (2002). Prosocial and helping behavior. In P. K. Smith & C. H. Hart (Eds.), *Blackwell handbook of childhood social development* (pp. 457-474). Malden, MA: Blackwell Publishing. Retrieved from http://www.pitt.edu/~toddlers/ESDL/Svetlova,etal_ToddlersProsocialBehavior.CDInPress09.pdf.

Hannah, F., & Meltzoff, A. N. (1993). Peer imitation by toddlers in laboratory, home, and day-care contexts: Implications for social learning and memory. *Developmental psychology, 29*, 701-710.

Halpern, L. F., MacLean, W. E., & Baumeister, A. A. (1995). Infant sleep-awake characteristics: Relation to neurological status and the prediction of developmental outcome. *Developmental review, 15*, 255-291.

Juffer, F., Bakersman-Kranenburg, M. J., & van IJzendoorn, M. H. (2004). Attachment-based intervention with video-feedback and biographical discussion: The Leiden VIPP and VIPP-R program. Hillsdale, NJ: Erlbaum.

Karns, C. M., Dow, M. W., & Neville, H. J. (2012). Altered cross-modal processing in the primary auditory cortex of congenitally deaf adults: A visual-somatosensory fMRI study with a double-flash illusion. *The Journal of Neuroscience, 32*(28), 9626-9638.

Lamb, M. (1994). Infant care practices and the application of knowledge. In C. B. Fisher & R. M. Learner (Eds.), *Applied Developmental Psychology* (pp. 23-45). New York, NY: McGraw-Hill.

Lund Jensen, L., Banner, J., Parm Ulhøi, B., & Byard, R. W. (4/22/2014). β-Amyloid precursor protein staining of the brain in sudden infant and early childhood death. *Neuropathology and Applied Neurobiology, 40*(4), 385-397.

McKenna, J. J., Mosko, S., Dungy, C., & McAninch, J. (1990). Sleep and arousal patterns of co-sleeping human mother/infant pairs:

A preliminary physiological study with implication for the study of sudden infant death syndrome (SIDS). *American Journal of Physical Anthropology, 83*, 331-347.

McKenna, J. J., Thoman, E. B., Anders, T. F., Sadeh, A., Schechtman, V. L., & Glotzbach, S. F. (1993). Infant-parent co-sleeping in an evolutionary perspective: Implications for understanding infant sleep development and the sudden infant death syndrome. *Sleep, 16*, 263-282.

Meltzoff, A. N. (1988). Infant imitation and memory: Nine-month-olds in immediate and deferred tests. *Child development, 59*, 217-225.

Mosko, S., Richard, C., & McKenna, J. (1997). Maternal sleep and arousals during bed sharing with infants. *Sleep, 20*(2), 142-150.

Nelson, S. & Schohl, A. (05/2010). Tool kit for children prenatally exposed. Macomb Intermediate School District, Clinton Township, Michigan. Retrieved from http://www.misd.net/earlyon/Prental Drug Exposure Tool Kit.pdf.

Neven, T. (reviewed 3/17/2014). Understanding postpartum depression – symptoms. Retrieved from http://www.webmd.com/depression/postpartum-depression.

Oxford Journals. (2000). *Journal of the National Cancer Institute, 92*(4), 302-312. Retrieved from http://jnci.oxfordjournals.org/content/92/4/302.full.

SIDS America (2011). Colorado Springs, Colorado. Retrieved from http://www.sidsamerica.org/sids-help/sids-support-groups.

Singleton, D., & Lengyel, Z. (1995). The age factor in second language acquisition: A *critical look at the critical period hypothesis,* 1-29. Clevedon, Bristol, UK: Multilingual Matters.

Sitskoorn, M. M., & Smitsman, A. W. (1995). Infants' perception of dynamic relations between objects: Passing through or supported? *Developmental Psychology, 31*, 437-447.

Sroufe, L. A., & Waters, E. (1976). The ontogenesis of smiling and laughter: A perspective on the organization of development in infancy. *Psychological Review, 83*, 173-189.

Wakschlag, L. S., Pickett, K. E., Cook, E., Jr, Benowitz, N. L., Bennett, L., & Leventhal, B. L. (2002). Maternal smoking during pregnancy and severe antisocial behavior in offspring: A review. *American Journal of Public Health, 92*(6), 966-974.

Warneken, F., & Tomasello, M. (2008). Extrinsic rewards undermine altruistic tendencies in 20-month-olds. *Developmental Psychology, 44*, 1785-1788. Retrieved from https://software.rc.fas.harvard.edu/lds.

Warneken, F., & Tomasello, M. (2012). Parental presence and encouragement do not influence helping in young children. *Infancy (Early View)*, 1-24. Retrieved from https://software.rc.fas.harvard.edu/lds.

Wolfe, P. (09/2011). The adolescent brain: a work in progress. Retrieved from http://patwolfe.com/2011/09/the-adolescent-brain-a-work-in-progress/.

Woolston, C. (n.d.). How smoking during pregnancy affects you and your baby. Retrieved from http://www.babycenter.com.

Infant and Toddler Further Reading

Academy of Nutrition and Dietetics (reviewed 01/2014). *Reducing the risk of food allergies*. Retrieved from http://www.eatright.org/Public/content.aspx?id=8052.

Allard, L. T., & Hunter, A. (10/2010). *Understanding temperament in infants and toddlers.* Center on the Social and Emotional Foundations for Early Learning. Vanderbilt University, Nashville, TN. Retrieved from http://csefel.vanderbilt.edu.

Bates, M. (2012). Super powers for the blind and deaf. *Scientific American*. Retrieved from http://www.scientificamerican.com/article/superpowers-for-the-blind-and-deaf/.

Bays, J., Emanuel Hospital, Portland, Oregon, 1986. McCullough, DeWoody, & Anderson (1993). ACT-2 Alcohol and other drugs: A competency-based training. Training for caregivers of AODexposed infants. CWLA, *Child Welfare Manual*. Fetal drug addiction. Retrieved from http://dss.mo.gov/cd/info/cwmanual.

Berlin, L. J., Ziv, Y., Amaya-Jackson, L., & Greenberg, M. T. (2005). *Enhancing early attachments: Theory, research, intervention, and policy*. New York, NY: Guilford.

Blakemore, C., & Ramirez, B. (n.d.). *Read aloud tips: Features of parentese*. Retrieved from http://www.readtoyourbaby.com.

Child Care Health and Development. (n.d.). *Texas A&M agrilife extension online*. Retrieved from http://extensiononline.tamu.edu/blog/.

Childproofing around the house. (n.d.). Retrieved from http://www.babycenter.com/0_childproofing-around-the-house_460.bc?page=2.

Cline, C. (n.d.). Interview with a world renowned potty training boys and potty training girls expert. Retrieved from http://www.pottytrainingboysgirls.org/.

Coping with sleep deprivation. (n.d.). Retrieved from http://www.babycenter.com/0_coping-with-sleep-deprivation_7968.bc?page=2.

Cohen, I. (n.d.). Bilingual babies: Teach your child a second language. *Parents Magazine*. Retrieved from http://www.parents.com/toddlers-preschoolers.

Desy, P. (n.d.). Are you getting enough zzz's? About.com. *Holistic Healing*. Retrieved from http://healing.about.com/od/sleepdisorders/a/are-you-getting-enough-sleep.htm.

Developing empathy: Raising children who care. (2014). Parenting Assistance Line. University of Alabama. Retrieved from http://www.pal.ua.edu/discipline.

Developmental milestones: Infant fine motor skills. (n.d.). Children's Therapy and family Resource Centre. British Columbia. Retrieved from http://www.kamloopschildrenstherapy.org.

Fine motor development 0 to 6 years: The development of fine motor skills. (2002). Retrieved from http://www.skillbuildersonline.com.

Gas in children. (n.d.). Retrieved from http://tummycalm.com.

Gavin, M. L. (reviewed 2011). Finger foods for babies. Nemours. Retrieved from http://kidshealth.org/parent/nutrition_center/healthy_eating/finger_foods.html#.

Gray, K. L. (2011). Effects of attachment on adjustment and friendship: Effects of parent-child attachment on social adjustment and friendship in young adulthood (Doctoral dissertation). Retrieved from http://digitalcommons.calpoly.edu.

Greene, A. (11/14/2013). Separation anxiety a-to-z guide from diagnosis to treatment to prevention. Retrieved from http://www.drgreene.com/articles/separation-anxiety.

Gross motor development & skills for infants, toddlers, and children. (n.d.). Early intervention support. Retrieved from http://www.earlyinterventionsupport.com/how-children-develop/gross-motor-skills-infants-toddlers-children.

Healthy sleep habits for infants and toddlers. (12/2013). Nationwide Children's Hospital. Retrieved from http://www.nationwidechildrens.org.

Holinger, P. C. (11/19/2012). Great kids, great parents: Infant/child development and the importance of children's feelings. *Psychology Today*. Retrieved from http://www.psychologytoday.com.

Lambert, S. R. (11/2007). Congenital rubella syndrome: the end is in sight. *The British Journal of Ophthalmology, 9*(11), 1418-1419. Retrieved from doi: 10.1136/bjo.2007.117960 or http://www.ncbi.nlm.nih.gov/pmc/articles/PMC2095420.

Marsh, B. (n.d.). Breast-feeding reduces cancer risk. Mail Online News. Retrieved from http://www.dailymail.co.uk/news/article-88785/Breast-feeding-reduces-cancer-risk.html.

Mayo Clinic Staff. (11/16/2011). *Potty training: How to get the job done*. Retrieved from http://www.mayoclinic.org/healthy-living/infant-and-toddler-health/in-depth/potty-training/art-20045230?pg=1.

Mendizza, M. (2014). *Sensory deprivation and the developing brain*. Infant massage usa. Retrieved from http://www.

infantmassageusa.org/research/articles-of-interest/sensory-deprivation-developing-brain.

Onderko, P. (n.d.). Crib sleeping vs co-sleeping: Where does your baby spend the night? *Parenting*. Retrieved from http://www.parenting.com/article/crib-sleeping-vs-co-sleeping.

Osborne, M. (10/24/2013). How does becoming blind affect other senses? Retrieved from http://www.livestrong.com/article/268986-how-does-becoming-blind-affect-other-senses.

Parker, R. & Hunter, C. (11/20/2011). Supporting couples across the transition to parenthood. Australian Institute of Family Studies. Retrieved from http://www.aifs.gov.au/cfca.

Saslow, D. (5/07/2013). *How is breastfeeding related to breast cancer?* American Cancer Society. Retrieved from http://www.cancer.org/search/index?QueryText=How+is+breastfeeding+related+to+breast+cancer%3F+.

Self Confidence (2012). Zero to three: National center for infants, toddlers, and families. Retrieved from http://main.zerotothree.org/site/PageServer?pagename=ter_par_1224_selfconfidence.

Springer, S. (1/12/2013). Marital happiness and the transition to parenthood: Do kids really kill a good marriage? *Psychology Today*. Retrieved from http://www.psychologytoday.com.

Sudden infant death syndrome: Australian study sheds new light. (4/17/2014). *The Financial Express*. Melbourne, Australia. Retrieved from http://www.financialexpress.com.

The first weeks home: Easing the new sibling transition. Nemours. Retrieved from http://kidshealth.org/parent/emotions/feelings/sibling_prep.html.

Todd, N. (3/17/2014 reviewed). Understanding Postpartum Depression – Symptoms. WebMD. http://www.webmd.com/depression/postpartum-depression.

Toma, John J., Ph.D. Neuropsychology. Biltmore Evaluation and Treatment Services. Phoenix, AZ.

Warren, D. H. (1996). Austin H. Riesen (1913-1996) Sensory deprivation pioneer. *Association for Psychological Sciences Observer*, 9(6). Retrieved from https://www.psychologicalscience.org.

Section 2

Early Childhood—
Ages Two through Six

Children's bodies grow straighter, stronger, and more coordinated during early childhood. Their brains develop, allowing them to begin to plan, communicate, and pay attention to what happens in their environment.

By age two, children may have a vocabulary of 200 words. They frequently have a vocabulary of 10,000 words by age six and will repeat everything they hear, making it important for parents and caregivers to use rich, varied language. Your vocabulary becomes theirs.

Preschoolers' scribbles begin to look like pictures. A child has the motor coordination to fully use the hand muscles by five, plus or minus two years. The child may be ready to wield a pencil as early as three or not until seven. Any age between three and seven is normal.

Two-year-olds typically either play alone or near other children with similar toys but not interacting with other children. Three-year-olds may share toys. Sharing should be encouraged, not forced. Toys are extensions of the child at this age. Forcing children to share their toys would be like forcing adults to hand their vehicles over to people they barely know, not knowing when they'd ever see their cars or trucks again. By four, many children are able to play cooperatively in small groups. They may work together to construct a block building or recreate a scene from home, with each child playing a different role. Children's play is based on what they see and experience in their environment. They need time to make up their own games and experience the give and take of other children. It is important for them to make their own discoveries and their own rules.

Many children between three and seven years of age have imaginary friends. Those children display more complex pretend play and are advanced in mental representation—a "picture" in the mind of an absent object or past event and are often more social with their peers (Taylor et al., 1993).

Preschool-aged children usually have high self-esteem. They believe they can do anything well, even if they haven't tried it yet. To help keep self-esteem at a high level, listen to the kids, notice their good work, accept their emotions, and choose your battles.

Young Children on Sharing

A wonderful, but unattributed, list of toddler's rules of sharing follows:
- If I like it, it's mine.
- If it's in my mouth, it's mine.
- If it's in my hand, it's mine.
- If I can take it away from you, it's mine.
- If I had it a little while ago, it's mine.
- If it's mine, it must not ever appear to be yours in any way.
- If I'm doing or building something, all of the pieces are mine.
- If it looks just like mine, it's mine.
- If I saw it first, it's mine.
- If you are playing with something and you put it down, it automatically becomes mine.
- If it's broken, it's yours.

Physical Development in Early Childhood

Brain Development

Early childhood, sometimes known as the play years, spans ages two to six. During this time, children add an average of two to three inches in height and about five pounds in weight per year. During early childhood, body fat lessens, the torso increases in size to make room for the internal organs, and the spine straightens, all causing the body to resemble an adult (Berk, 2002).

Although the brain has a surplus of synapses initially, a period of heavy pruning begins around age three. By age four, children's brain metabolism reaches a peak well above that of an adult's brain. During early childhood, many areas of the brain have an extra supply of synapses, which increases a need for energy. Many synapses have the same jobs. This is helpful in case some of those synapses are damaged. Lightly used nerve cells lose their connective fibers, and the number of synapses lessens. Energy usage of children's brains nears adult level by age eight or nine (Chugani, 1994).

Right and Left Hemisphere Specialization

The frontal lobe, the area of the brain that involves planning and organizing behavior, grows rapidly from age three to six. The left side of the brain, which controls math and reasoning skills, is highly active during this time. The cerebellum, a structure at the back and base of the brain, helps with balance and control of body movement. This area is fully myelinated by about age four. The right hemisphere is a pattern recognizer. It enables a child to attend to and appreciate sensory experience. The brain structure that controls attention, the reticular formation, continues growth into adolescence, which explains how the ability to pay attention increases as time progresses (McGuinness & Pribram, 1980). The developing brain enables children to begin to plan, communicate, and pay attention to what happens in their environment.

Verbal skills may be found in either hemisphere. The majority of males process language in the left hemisphere. Most females process language in both left and right hemispheres.

The corpus callosum connects the left and right sides of the brain. The connection allows communication to flow from one hemisphere to the other. It is fairly developed by age five and continues to grow through adolescence. At one time, it was thought that the corpus callosum was a structure that kept the hemispheres of the brain connected to each other with no other purpose. Without this structure, the left side would not know what the right side was doing. The corpus callosum allows each hemisphere to specialize, allowing one specialized half to suppress the actions of the other—language for instance (Toma, 2014).

The brain is fascinating. At one time it was thought human beings only used a small portion of the brain. Now we know this is not accurate. Certain areas have specific functions, which have already been mapped out. All areas of the brain are responsive. Even during sleep and daydreaming, many areas of the brain are activated.

Motor Skills in Early Childhood

Young children want to help themselves.

"I do it, Mommy!"

"Two year olds put on and take off simple clothing. By age 3, they . . . take care of toileting needs by themselves. Between ages 4 and 5, children can dress and undress without supervision" (Berk, 2002, p. 312).

If a child can remove a toy from a box, she can also put the toy away. Items may not be placed as quickly or exactly as a parent might prefer, but "I do it" is a great time to teach clean up. If started early in life and in a positive manner, clean up time will not be argument-filled torture time. The best method I know, which I wish I had thought of for my own children, is to have a specific time and day for family clean up. Everyone participates as they are able by age. When the house is clean, the family goes out and does something fun. The anticipation of family fun makes clean up seem to go faster. Since everyone is helping at the same time, clean up feels fair—an important issue for young children.

Clean-up Time
(author unknown)

Clean-up, clean-up
Everybody everywhere,
Clean-up, clean-up
Everybody do their share.

Other clean-up songs are on the web, with several on YouTube. Singing seems to make clean up go faster.

Parenting... A Work in Progress

Two and three-year-olds are capable of putting toys back in a container.

- Make the request with a cheerful voice.
- Clean with the child; the task will seem less daunting.
- Be consistent.
- Clean up will become habit.

Children's Art

Children as young as eighteen months can make marks on paper with crayons. Supervision is vital, as their artwork may move from paper to wall. When my first child was two, she created a glorious mural on the kitchen wall. It was five feet long and as tall as she could reach. She was incredibly fast. Fortunately, WD-40 worked like a charm.

By age three, children's scribbles begin to look like pictures. Some children have very specific ideas as to what the picture should look like. They see it in the mind, but it doesn't translate on paper. They become frustrated.

> Lynn handed her mother a drawing. Mother had no clue what she was looking at.
> "Tell me about your picture Lynn."
> "It's lil mermaid!"
> "Oh, it's the Little Mermaid from your book. It's beautiful!"
> Lynn looked at her mother with three-year-old disbelief. "No butiful, Mommy. You do it."
> "No Lynn. This is your art. If I do it, then it's my art. I love your art!"
> Lynn smiled at her mother and reached out to hug her. "I do it, Mommy."

Not all three-year-olds are as intent as Lynn. More accurate drawing occurs gradually, with practice and encouragement into the school-age years. Some children are very serious and sensitive about their artwork. When a parent is unsure what the child has drawn, it is

Early Childhood—Ages Two through Six

better to say "Tell me about your picture" than "What is it?" to the artist-in-training.

A child has the motor coordination to fully use the hand muscles by five, plus or minus two years. The child may be ready to wield a pencil as early as three or not until seven. Any age between three and seven is considered normal.

Encourage preschoolers to draw their ideas and feelings rather than fill in and color pre-drawn shapes and forms. Ask them to tell you about their pictures. The children's explanations will give insight about what is going on in their minds.

Markers are bright, colorful, easy to use, and sometimes smell good enough to eat. They should be used sparingly. Crayons provide more friction than markers. The effort required strengthens the muscles needed for fine motor skills. If young children primarily use markers, when they arrive in kindergarten, they will complain of muscle fatigue.

Activities to Strengthen Hand Muscles:

- Play Dough – Use in a non-carpeted area. It is difficult to remove from the rug.

Play Dough Recipe

3 cups water
1 cup salt
2 teaspoons food coloring, or a packet of powdered drink mix
4 tablespoons alum (found in the spice section of the grocery store)
4 tablespoons vegetable oil
3 cups flour

Heat the water and salt in a large sauce pan, and bring to a rolling boil. Boil for two minutes. Remove from heat.

Add other ingredients. The mixture will be hot, so stir with a long-handled spoon until able to knead it with your hands. It will start out lumpy. Knead until smooth and glossy. If the mixture feels crumbly after kneading, add a bit more oil and knead it in. When completely cool, store in a closed container. A zippered plastic bag will work. The container may be refrigerated, but it's not necessary.

Homemade play dough usually lasts for a month.

- Modeling Clay – More difficult to work with than play dough. Use for more resistance.
- Scissors – Blunted children's scissors require a squeezing motion. Start with straight lines, such as fringing the edges of a paper bag.
- Clothes Pins – Good for pincer grasp, used later for writing.
- Pizza or Bread Dough – Fun to squeeze, punch, pull, poke after it rises, spread in a pan, and eat after it's cooked.

Recipe for Edible Dough

1 18-ounce jar of smooth nut butter (peanut, almond, cashew, hazelnut)
¾ cup nonfat dried milk
6 tablespoons honey (safe for children two and older)

Mix honey with nut butter. Add dried milk until of dough consistency. Pinch off pieces. Roll into logs and form letters, words, or shapes. Eat.

Letter Reversals

Children commonly reverse letters, especially before first grade. Letters that are mirror images of each other are difficult for children to tell apart. For example, it is common to see confusion over letters "b" and "d."

To help with beginning spelling at home:
- Try saying, "It's time for b-e-d." Then send the children to bed.
- Try drawing a tiny mattress over the printed word "bed" to help them remember where the circles in the letters go. This will help the children remember the correct order of letters.
- Make letters on a table using shaving cream.
- Form words in pudding spread out on a sheet of waxed paper.
- Show children how to form letters/words in the air with their index finger.
- Form letters/words in the sand with hands and feet.
- Make and eat your name with edible dough.

For any activity with young children, focus on the fun, not the form. Breathe deeply. Enjoy the children's enthusiasm. It is contagious.

Play and Self-Esteem in Early Childhood

Types of Play

Children's play is based on what they see and experience in their environment.

Between two and five, play goes through several stages:
- Solitary play—when a child plays by himself or herself.
- Parallel play—in which a child plays near other children with similar toys but does not interact with the other children.
- Associative play—when children share toys and verbally interact while engaging in different activities.
- Cooperative play—in which children work together for a common goal, like make-believe grocery store, or working together to make a product, like constructing a building of blocks.

By four, many children are capable of cooperative play. Older children use all forms of play, from solitary to cooperative. Each situation requires flexibility in the type of play chosen. The child's comfort level with the immediate environment and playmates determines the play type.

Play helps children make sense of the world around them. Children imitate what they see.

> Two-year-old Ashley surprised her parents when she said, "I go work," and then climbed on a chair in the home office and banged on the computer keyboard.

Every day Ashley watched her parents use the computer. She imitated the adults in her life and "went to work" as they did.

A different play was acted out in the reading area of a preschool classroom:

> One four-year-old boy put a baby doll under his shirt and lay down on the floor. Another classmate sat on the floor next to his "pregnant" friend and gently rubbed his friend's tummy and said, "You'll be okay."

Both children's families had recently increased in number. The children acted out what they saw at home.

> Five-year-old Peyton tapped her foot repeatedly on the floor of the housekeeping area of the classroom, play telephone in her hand.
> "Husband, husband, get home now!" stated Peyton loudly.

Peyton acted out a scene from part of her life. She imitated what she heard, perhaps attempting to understand or make sense of what she experienced. Repetition of actions from home are commonly acted out in the preschool classroom. Children do not miss a thing.

An eighteen-month-old child will use an empty cup and pretend to drink. The same child will pick up a toy telephone and talk to someone. By age two, children will use an object to substitute for something else, like using a block for the telephone. Sometime during the third year, children may involve imaginary objects or friends in play.

Imaginary Friends

According to Laura Berk, one fourth to almost half of children between three and seven years of age have imaginary friends. Those children display more complex pretend play, are advanced in mental representation, and are often more social with their peers.

Dictated Stories

By four, children can dictate imaginative stories to an adult, choose characters, ask friends to have a specific part in the story, and then act out the story in front of their peers. The four- and five-year-old preschool students in the following stories acted out their peer's dictated stories.

The first child named in the list of story characters dictated the story to the teacher. The child also helped determine who the characters in the story would be and asked his peers to be characters in the story when it was read and performed. If the peer said "no, thank you," the "author" asked another student to be in the story until all characters were chosen.

> **Buster and Babs**
>
> Buster – Kristofer (also the author of the story)
> Babs – Aaren
> Baby T-Rex – Mrs. E.
> Big Dinosaur – Mrs. B
> Fur-ball - Eileen
>
> I was making a dinosaur egg, and then it hatched a baby Tyrannosaurus rex. And then I was scared, and I was running. But Babs liked him. Then she said, "I go on a airplane."
> Then I said, "I hate flying."
> Then I was shock. Then I was felt goin' round and round. And then I saw a big dinosaur. Babs run away, and I pet him.
> And then she goes on a airplane and she said, "I hate flying. I hate flying."
> And then I was playing with my toys and puzzles with Babs. And then mine was so cute. Then I was playing Mousetrap with Babs. And then something came and scared me. I was so really, really, really scared 'cause Fur-ball came. And then I was so tired on

Parenting...A Work in Progress

> the airplane. Then I felt like watching Nick Arcade 'cause I got up so early. The end.

In her story, "The Missing Mushroom," Samantha asked Andy to be Brother and Lisa to be Sister. The teacher read the play as the characters moved according to the words in Samantha's story.

> **The Missing Mushroom**
>
> Mom – Samantha
> Brother – Andy
> Sister – Lisa
>
> All the persons came to the person's house. And at the person's house they were hunting for the mushrooms. Then they had a garden. They looked in the mushroom garden but there wasn't any mushrooms.
>
> And then when all the people left, the mom and the brother and the sister looked in the refrigerator. And then they found some mushrooms, and they put the mushrooms in a pot. And they put water in it and some orange juice.
>
> And then the sister went out and she tripped on a rock and fell and hurt herself. And then they found a flower on the rock. The end.

"The Rainforest," dictated to the teacher by Ryan, was shorter than some of the other stories but flowed smoothly for a child so young. It also included cooperation and kindness, qualities stressed in the classroom.

> **The Rainforest**
>
> Lion – Ryan
> Wife Lion – Mrs. B
> Baby Cub – Andy
> Bear – Josh
>
> Once upon a time, there lived a lion. He went into

> his house looking for his wife. She was in the kitchen with her new baby cub.
>
> A bear came into their house. The bear became friends with the lion family. And every time they needed a babysitter they could count on the bear and the bear could count on the lions. The end.

The differences in the students' storytelling abilities were remarkably large. Early in the school year the language used in dictated stories was sparse with limited vocabulary. As the year progressed so did the stories, which became more complex in wording and more organized in thought.

Mini Dramas

The following mini-drama was dictated by a five-year-old student without character choices.

> Once upon a time there lived Miss Piggy. And Miss Piggy wanted to go to Africa. But she couldn't go to Africa because there was no planes to go there. All the planes were all filled up.
>
> So, she decided to go the China because there was planes there. So she drove to China. And the planes were all empty. And then she went to China. And at China she saw that the planes were all empty.
>
> And at China she took a picture when she was leaving in the plane. And when she was there, she saw Kermit. And Kermit said, "Why don't we go to the library to get some books?"
>
> Miss Piggy said, "No." And then she said, "Because you just get to borrow them for one day."
>
> So then she said, "Why don't we go to the bookstore where you can keep the books?"
>
> So they went to the bookstore. And then Miss Piggy found a book called "Around the World in Eighty Days."
>
> She said to Kermit, "My brother watched the movie

> once."
>
> And Kermit got a book too. And it was called "What Do You Think?"
>
> And Kermit said to Miss Piggy, "What book do you have?"
>
> She said, "Around the World in Eighty Days."
>
> He said, "Oh."
>
> And Miss Piggy said, "What book do you have?"
>
> He said, "What Do You Think?"
>
> "Why won't you tell me?" she said.
>
> And then he said, "Okay, I'll tell you. What Do You Think?"
>
> The End

Participating in this type of activity shows children that their words may be written down and read. The written words have meaning. The story is important to them because it is in their own words. If a child writing his name is his first stamp on the world, imagine how meaningful his stories must be.

Suggestions to Enhance Make-Believe Play

- Have a specific play space. A portion of the child's bedroom or other specified area where toys have a "home."
- Laundry baskets or crates are handy for toy storage and make it easier for children to pick up their playthings when it is time to clean up.
- Use dress-up clothes, trucks, toy scenes, wooden or plastic blocks, cardboard cylinders from paper towel rolls, paper or cloth bags, and cardboard boxes to encourage make-believe play.
- Join in play if you are asked. If the child is playing veterinarian's office, the parent may be asked to be one of the pets.

> Kaitlyn had several stuffed toy animals on the bed and held a stethoscope from her toy doctor's bag in her hand. She heard her mother walk by her bedroom.
>
> "Mommy, you be the dog."
>
> Mother, on the way to her home office, stopped in Kaitlyn's doorway. "Okay, email can wait a few minutes. Where do you want me to go?"
>
> "Over there, by the table." Kaitlyn pointed to the corner of her room.
>
> Mother looked around in confusion. "What table? I don't see a table."
>
> "Here, Mommy-doggy! I'll walk you there. No Mommy, I walk. You walk like doggy."
>
> Kaitlyn took Mommy-doggy's paw and walked to the corner of her room. The table was invisible. "Doggy, you sick. Oh, oh. Doggy, you dead. Lie down doggy, you dead."
>
> Two minutes passed and Kaitlyn was busy talking to people on her vet's office phone. Mother sat up. "No, no, doggy. You still dead!"
>
> "Kaitlyn, in two more minutes Mommy has to finish reading email. As soon I'm done I'll come back and see how your patients are doing."
>
> "Okay Mommy-doggy. Lay down. You dead!"

Expensive play-sets can be fun but are not necessary for make-believe. The greatest gift you can give to children is time. Time set aside for play with friends and family members may help keep children's feelings about themselves positive. The greatest gift you can give to children is time. Show children they are important to you by entering their world of play.

The Art of Sharing

Young children are often firm about their belongings or those items they believe belong to them. Recall the childhood cheers, "It's Mine!" or "Everything is mine unless it's broken. Then it's yours."

Although self-assertion is a good thing, children also need to learn the fine arts of redirection and compromise.

- *"It's your friend's turn to use the toy in five minutes."* Children of this age have no conceptual understanding of time, so they require adult help. Use either a timer or a verbal reminder to switch. Beware hourglass toy timers. A savvy child may turn the timer upside down when no one is looking to get more playtime.
- *"Here is a different toy. See if your friend will trade."* Trades frequently work well. However, sometimes the trade is not enticing, and a different trade may be attempted. If this method fails, it is time to find a different play option.

These methods encourage cooperation rather than insist upon immediate sharing, which is a supreme difficulty for young children. The toys, for the time they are in hand, are extensions of the self. Instead of insisting a child share or physically removing a toy from one child to give to another, use of these two techniques will teach children good compromising strategies.

Self-Esteem

Preschool aged children usually have high self-esteem. They believe they can do anything well, even if they haven't tried it yet. Kindergarten-aged children believe that feelings are emotional expression. If a friend is smiling, he is happy. When a friend is not smiling she is not happy (Nanis & Cowen, 1987).

Suggestions for maintaining healthy self-esteem:

- Listen. Give your full attention when children want to talk. If you listen to your children now, they will return the favor and listen to you later. Young children have little problems.

Early Childhood—Ages Two through Six

Older children have bigger problems. They need to be assured you will be available for them when they need you.
- Promote self-motivation. Notice the positive in the child's behavior and accomplishments above and beyond, saying "Good job." Display their work.
- Accept the child's emotions. Let the child know it is okay to be angry, but it's not okay to treat other people badly because of that anger. Try saying, "Smart girls or boys find a way to fix problems." Help the child calm down so he can think of a constructive way to handle the situation. If he can't think of a solution, offer suggestions so the child feels supported.
- Pick your battles. Children need to feel they have some control over their lives. This will help them learn to make their own decisions—a necessary life-skill.

> Daughter Julia had a unique sense of fashion. "Thank goodness her school required uniforms," her father stated, after Julia walked past him wearing a white and purple striped shirt and pants with large printed flowers.
>
> Outside of school, Julia was allowed to wear what she wished, as long as it was weather appropriate—no shorts in the dead of winter. No matter how extreme the clash of the clothing, we let it go. Clothing choice would not be a battle. She was expressing her creativity.
>
> On days when Julia was required to dress for a more formal outing, I chose two outfits. Julia chose one and wore that outfit. She was always given a choice.
>
> Now an adult, Julia has no difficulties making decisions in her technical position at work. She designs and constructs purses and clothing for fun.

Listen, promote self-motivation, accept emotions, and choose your battles. If you parent well now, your children will not need you to continue parenting them into their adult years. Children who never learn to make their own decisions have difficulty making decisions as an adult.

Behavior in Public in Early Childhood

Children need guidance to know how to behave. They learn what to do where and with whom while observing the people around them and by direct instruction. Children learn that grandma expects better manners than cousin does. They adjust behavior accordingly.

Stores

Children learn at an early age what they can get away with in public.

> A father walked through a toy store with his three-year-old daughter. He planned to purchase diapers for his newborn son. He brought his daughter shopping to give Mom a much-needed break. The daughter sat in the cart and looked at all the colorful toys. She wanted a toy pony in the worst way.
>
> The daughter reached her hands toward the ponies on a shelf. Her father told her "no," and pushed the cart farther down the aisle, still looking for diapers.
>
> She screamed at her father, "I want pony. I want pony!" His face reddened while other shoppers stared at him and his daughter. She continued screaming.
>
> Dad, embarrassed and unable to deal with her tantrum, turned the cart around, grabbed a My Little Pony, and gave it to his daughter. "Here, is that better? Now be quiet."
>
> Daughter, happy with the pony, was quiet for the rest of the trip.

I had a similar experience with one of my children in a department store.

> With a limited budget, I could afford only what I needed. My two-year-old daughter sat in the shopping cart and looked at the toys as we passed them.
>
> "Winnie Poo, Winnie Poo," she yelled as we passed the bright yellow bear.
>
> "Sorry, we can't buy him. Mommy doesn't have enough money."
>
> "Winnie Poo, Winnie Poo!" she screamed, arms reaching toward the bear.
>
> People all over the store stared at us. I chose to ignore them, but it was not easy. Seeing that she was not going to stop yelling for Pooh bear, I had to decide whether to let her have the bear or pick her up and leave the store. I opted to leave without purchasing anything.
>
> My daughter cried while I lifted her out of the cart. She flailed her arms and legs. It became necessary to hold her at my side encircled by my arm, the football hold. Her arms and legs hit the air instead of me or anyone that may have come near. No one came close.
>
> "We're going home," I told her.
>
> Shoppers stared after us. It didn't matter.

I worried that, if I'd given in and bought the bear, it would have been the beginning of a bad trend. If I gave in, anytime she wanted something and didn't get it, she'd scream, knowing from experience that screaming would produce the result she wanted.

It was her only tantrum in public.

Before my children were old enough to enjoy shopping, I devised a method to ensure good shopping behavior. If they were patient while shopping, we might go to the cinnamon roll store in the mall. I didn't want them to think they would always get a treat, which is why I used the word "might." Around every third shopping trip, we stopped at the cinnamon roll store and bought a small treat. To make sure it worked, the first time they were good at the mall, we went for a treat to reinforce good behavior.

Some children's senses are easily overloaded, making long shopping trips seem perilous to them and a tantrum risk. Too many people. Too much emotion. They feel stuck in a whirlwind of sights and sounds, yelling to get out.

Strategies

Consider the following:
- Make the trips short.
- Give a five- or ten-minute warning before leaving home.
- Inform the child in advance of the plan for the outing.
- Have the child use the bathroom before leaving the house.
- Bring a snack.

These suggestions are helpful for all children, but are particularly important for children who are learning social skills or have sensory issues.

Restaurants

I brought my children with me everywhere I went. I felt it important for children to experience life first hand as much as possible. We went to museums, community concerts, and restaurants together.

When I was young, my brothers and I went to restaurants with our parents. If another child in the restaurant misbehaved, we were told, "If you ever act like that, you'll never go to restaurants. So behave yourselves."

I preferred to stress the positive. We told our children how wonderful they were and how happy we were to take them places.

Many restaurants are child friendly, offering crayons and paper to keep children occupied while waiting for food. If I knew in advance a restaurant did not have paper and crayons, I brought them with me. Some restaurants have a connected indoor play area, so children can get some exercise and burn off extra energy while they wait for their meal or after they finish eating. Others have games that may be played at the table. Some children bring electronic devices to keep themselves occupied.

Children do not do well seated in one spot for an extended time because it is physically uncomfortable for them. Some wiggling should be expected. Squirming in the seat is an indication the child needs to get up and move around. Have him stand up and walk over to someone else at the table to stretch some muscles.

> Rafael, a waiter, had this to say. "When I see a family coming to one of my tables, I make sure there are crackers for the kids. They can get hungry and loud. The crackers help a lot. What really annoys me is when the adults ignore the kids. The kids get up and start running around the restaurant. That situation isn't safe for anyone. The waiters try not to trip and spill trays full of food on the customers. I want to say something, but I can't."

When children misbehave in restaurants, other patrons sometimes give the "hairy eyeball" to the children's parents. My husband and I have taken to complimenting the parents of children who are using good restaurant behavior. Parents and children need to know when they are being awesome.

Most people enjoy going out to eat. Someone else makes the food, pours the coffee, and asks if there is anything required at the table. If adult time is needed, have a date night without the kids. Don't feel guilty. Parents should remember to take breaks. Parenting is a difficult job.

Strategies

When going out as a family, do just that. One of the reasons children run around in a public place is to get attention. It's better to give positive attention, letting your children know how proud you are of them when they're behaving well, than to give negative attention by yelling at them for running around. Catch them being good, and reward them with praise.

Parenting... A Work in Progress

    Consistency is paramount. Children need to know their parents' rules. Parents should determine the behavior they want their children to exhibit. A two-year-old will not understand about lack of funds, but will learn what his parents expect through the constant testing of parental limits. Children's behavior will rise to their parents' expectations.

Discovery Learning in Early Childhood

Discovery Learning

> The preschool teacher set up the classroom with areas of activities based on the interests of the students. Early in the school year, he presented the children, aged four to five, with a school drawn on a poster board. The preschoolers took turns drawing pictures of what they wanted to learn.
>
> Kevin walked into the classroom. He was the first student to arrive. He hugged his mother, then walked immediately to the science area. Kevin's mother smiled. "He doesn't care if I'm here or gone. Kevin has really grown to love his preschool."
>
> "Yes, Mrs. Smith. Kevin really enjoys himself in class."
>
> Kevin yelled from the other side of the classroom. "Mr. Barry I figured out your experiment!"
>
> "Mrs. Smith, do you want to see what Kevin's talking about?"
>
> "I'd love to, but I have to take my older son to school." Mrs. Smith looked towards the science area and smiled at her son. "Kevin, be good!"
>
> "Bye, Mom. Teacher, come see."
>
> The teacher walked to the far side of the classroom to see what Kevin had discovered.
>
> On the science table the teacher had placed the following:

Parenting... A Work in Progress

> Two bowls, one filled half-way with water, one empty.
> Two large bath towels to soak up excessive spills.
> Three sponges: two natural sponges of differing sizes and one large cellulose kitchen sponge.
> Kevin pointed at the three sponges on the small round science table. "I think this big, bumpy sponge will hold the most water. I think it's about which sponge is best."
> "Kevin, you are so smart! Do you want to test your guess, or do you want to wait for your friends to get here?"
> "I can wait. Look, there's Sammy. Hi, Sammy!" Kevin began running to the cubby area of the classroom, where Sammy was hanging up his jacket.
> "Use walking feet, please. Thank you, Kevin."

The children will remember the last action word in a command or request. If an adult says, "Don't run," the child will hear and remember the word "run" and then proceed to run through the room. Better to say, "Walk, please," or "Use walking feet," so the child will walk. Avoid negatives whenever possible.

The teacher did not have a set agenda for science that day. This was purely a time for discovery learning. Much knowledge may be gained in this type of exploratory lesson. It involves action, cooperation, and discussion.

"There is no screaming in science!"

> The day arrived to take the magnifying glasses to the playground to observe tiny living things. The teachers wanted to increase the children's vocabulary level. They used the term "observe." Each child took a magnifying glass outside, running around busily with and without their friends. The grand search was afoot!

> Two of the children ran to their teacher, Ms. B, and yelled, "The ants are marching!" Ms. B walked with them to see the marching ants. They looked closely and noticed how the ants seemed to walk in lines, one following the other, just like the students lined up, but with less noise.
>
> Suddenly Matthew screamed. The people in the schoolyard stopped whatever they were doing to find out who was screaming and why. Ms. B ran to Matthew to determine the cause of his hurt. There was no blood, no bruise, and no hurt feelings. Ms. B got a moistened paper towel to put where he was pointing. By then he was too hysterical to say what happened. Finally, after applying the towel, Matthew told his teacher that an ant was crawling on his leg. Apparently the ant had bitten Matthew a few times on its journey.
>
> Several other children came to find out what had happened to their friend. After seeing that he was unharmed, the hunt for tiny living things continued. Matthew quickly got over his ant bites and continued the search as well.

Several students expressed concern for a fellow classmate, exhibiting empathy, which was stressed in Ms. B's classroom. Activities done outdoors have fewer controls but offer more opportunities for excitement.

Early Literacy

> Christine, Larry, and two-year-old Justin rode in their car. In the back, Justin wiggled in his car seat.
>
> "Mommy, fries!" Justin said, pointing at the large yellow M on a billboard at the side of the road.
>
> "Who took you there, Justin?" asked both parents.
>
> "Gamma, Papa," said Justin, blissfully looking out the car window.

> Christine's jaw dropped. "Larry, your parents know we don't give Justin fast food!"

Justin "read" the yellow "M" on the billboard and related it to what he had eaten. He was constructing literacy knowledge through informal experience. In this case, the big yellow "M" meant fries.

Children's Private Speech

Preschoolers often speak aloud to themselves, like a running dialogue, talking about what they do as they play and explore. Talking to the self helps children think about what they are doing. This self-dialogue or self-talk happens more frequently when the task is new to them or difficult. It is the beginning stage of learning to self-regulate attention and concentration.

As children get older, their audible self-speech transitions to whispered speech, then to silent lip movement.

Mathematical Reasoning

Children begin to count between ages two and three, first by memorizing the words. A three-year-old child may display how old she is by holding up fingers. Initially, she may hold up two fingers while saying she is three. If she practices with an adult or other more advanced peer, she will consistently hold up the correct number of fingers.

Young children constantly compare themselves with their friends. Who runs faster? Who is bigger? They encounter measurement everyday as they explore and make sense of their environment (Copley, 2000).

> Dad plunked a candy bar on the countertop. "Okay, kids, this candy bar is really big, so the three of you will share it. Ellen, you're the oldest, so your job is to divide it up into three pieces. Oh, and remember, the person who does the dividing picks last." Dad got a beverage from the fridge and left.

> Ellen, eight years old, unwrapped the candy while her younger brothers, Bill, who was four, and Mikey, two and a half, crowded their sister. Drool spilled from Mikey's mouth. "Just a second, you guys." She reached for the child-safe knife her father left on the counter. Mikey grabbed the candy and ran off. "Quick, Bill, catch Mikey. He'll eat it all and get sick. Remember what happened last Easter?"
> Bill ran after his baby brother.
> Mikey, less coordinated than Bill, was caught in the time span of a few heartbeats. The candy bar was still in one piece.
> "Thanks, Bill." Ellen cut the candy bar in three pieces as evenly as possible. Both boys grabbed a third. Ellen, the divider, chose last.

Ellen had a basic understanding of division. Her frontal lobe, at age eight, had developed enough to understand abstract concepts. Her brother Bill didn't understand the concept of division but knew same size meant fair. Mikey was just interested in treats.

Mathematical vocabulary is easy to explain by action and simultaneous word use. "Divide the candy" means cut it into parts. In this case, the parts were meant to be equal. The children understood and knew what to expect according to their developmental ability.

Hands-on discovery learning is the fastest method children use to learn. Many children are full-body kinesthetic learners—in other words, they use their bodily senses to gain experience. Children will have a greater understanding of a concept if they are given the opportunity to "play" and learn without constant adult supervision. Watching from a short distance is good. Hovering is not necessary and may interfere with knowledge acquisition.

Thinking in Preschool

During group time, four- and five-year-old preschool students were asked to think of their favorite food and how to prepare it.

The teacher took her students to the writing area of the classroom. The students dictated the name of their favorite food, along with ingredients and cooking instructions. It was an enlightening experience for parents and teachers.

Here are some recipes:

> **Chocolate Chip Cookies by Michelle**
> Mix together butter, flour, and chocolate chips. Put flour on Mom's head. Put them in the oven for a long time. Let them cool off after they're done. Eat them.
>
> **Steak by Bryan**
> Cook on the grill. I like it black. Then put on barbeque sauce.
>
> **Cake by Ricky**
> Roast beef, cheese
> You cook it in the refrigerator for five minutes. The cake is really good.
>
> **Cookie Muffins by Swen**
> First you have to stir the cookies around. And then, when the red light goes off you do it. Then you put the muffin makers in the muffin maker things. And then when you are all done put a spoon into the muffin. Muffin goes into the spoon. And then when we are already done, put them in the muffin maker and then the oven. I like cookie muffins. They are very hot, but just wait.

> **Sugar Cookies by Ashley**
> Mix sugar, grinded up strawberries, flour, and butter, and a little bit of onion. Mix together. Sprinkle sugar on top. Put in oven on a cookie sheet and cook for twenty hours. Eat them.
>
> **Cookies by Patrick**
> You buy it from the store. Then you put it on the dough thing. Then you let it cook in the oven for four hours. Then you let it cool on the paper towel. And when it flatten, then you eat it.

The location for cooking—should food cook in the oven or the refrigerator?—is an area of confusion, as is time.

Time Out

One of the preschool parents relayed a situation about time-out limits at home.

> "I realized Susan had no understanding of time when I told her she would have a fifteen- minute time-out and she said to me, 'Oh no! That's more than one hour!' and started to cry."
>
> Mom had previously given her four-year-old daughter a long time out, not understanding children's limited attention span. Her daughter understood the number fifteen is larger than the number one, but Susan did not understand the difference between minutes and hours. To her, fifteen minutes sounded like forever. She was understandably distraught.

Time to Think About It

Thinking time, a form of time-out, may be used to help a child learn self-control and self-regulate, a good skill for life. When a child has difficulty controlling himself, yelling at him will not help. It might vent some adult steam, but even that is temporary. Try the following:

- Take a step back; this gives physical space and a few seconds to think.
- Inhale, then exhale slowly. Breathing slowly relaxes the mind and lowers blood pressure. Voluntary slow deep breathing resets the autonomic nervous system and decreases the effects of stress (S. Novotny & L. Kravitz, 2007).
- Count to ten audibly. Counting aloud allows for adult thinking-time and lets the child know you are unhappy and ready for serious discussion.
- Lower your body position so you are at the child's level. Eye-to-eye position ensures everyone is paying attention and listening, not just hearing
- Ask the child what happened. Sometimes the fault lies with others.
- Give the child alternatives to her actions. If she wanted a toy and grabbed it from someone, an alternative would be to trade a different toy instead of just taking a toy from another child.
- Ask the child to repeat what happened and why the parent is unhappy. Memory is fleeting, and the child needs reminding to remember.
- If necessary, use thinking time—a short time away from family and friends.

Use a soft item for the child to sit in: beanbag chair, cushion, or other place for repose in a quiet area of the home for thinking time.

- Let the child know he may resume playing after he has finished thinking time and has spoken with the parent.
- Make sure the child knows she will be missed while she is away.
- Saying sorry is not enough. The word sorry must be accompanied by something meaningful, which requires thought.
- Thinking time should only last a few minutes for young children. If he is taking too long, check on him and talk about what he is thinking.
- Let her know she should come back when she is ready.

Thinking time is time away from the rest of family and friends. Parents who choose to use this method may discover their children eventually put themselves in thinking time when they feel the need. It is an excellent way to help children learn to self-regulate. According to a study by the University of Pennsylvania, the ability to self-regulate—to pay attention and control behavior—is the best predictor of math and reading ability in kindergarten.

"Why do fish swim?"

> In a preschool classroom, students learned about fish. In the science area of the classroom, the teacher placed a ten-gallon aquarium with three fish: two tetras named Greenish and Orangie after their colored stripe, and one plecostomus named Plico. All the children enjoyed watching the fish move about their aquarium home.
>
> Greenish and Orangie swam in a manner the children expected. Plico was different. Plico, a sucker fish, spent most days attached to the sides of the glass, eating algae, and showing off the insides of his mouth. The students decided Plico was a he, and both Greenish and Orangie were girl-fish.
>
> The four- and five-year-old students were asked to observe the fish and then draw pictures of what the fish did during the day. One interesting question was raised. Why do fish swim? Some answers follow:
>
> Because if they couldn't swim, they wouldn't live. – Hannah
>
> Because their tails wag, and because their stomachs move and their stomachs make their fins move. – Annie
>
> You know why they swim? Because they have fins and they can poop. – Jack
>
> Cause they need to fly. – Taylor
>
> Because if they didn't swim, they can't breathe. - Ali
>
> Cause they don't have any legs. - Haley

Young children do not view the world the same way adults do. Some have prior knowledge from family; some have understanding through observation in the classroom; others either didn't have any idea, or made up answers. Children's depth of thinking is shaped by life experiences. Exposure to the arts and sciences, particularly hands-on activities, supplies children with a rich palette to use for future thought and understanding.

Nutrition in Early Childhood

"I don't want it. I don't like it."

Preschoolers' appetites are unpredictable. Children who would try anything at age two may become picky eaters at three. The amount of food eaten from meal to meal can vary dramatically, depending on age, body size, energy expended, growth rate, and appetite.

Children need the same healthy foods that adults eat but in smaller amounts. Some fat is needed in a healthy diet. Without fat, Vitamins A, D, E, and K—all fat-soluble vitamins—cannot be absorbed and used by the body.

Foods high in sugar contribute to tooth decay and fill children up, lessening their appetite for healthy foods. A relaxed mealtime adds enjoyment and aids digestion. Power struggles over food cause unnecessary stress to the whole family and interfere with food absorption.

> Jason entered the preschool classroom with his mother, Jennifer, earlier than usual that morning. The teacher, Ms. Bartlett, was in the art area, mixing paint extender with pigment for the students to use for the day.
>
> "Good morning, Mrs. Jaines. Jason, come over and help me pick paint colors."
>
> Jason and his mother walked to the back of the classroom where Ms. Bartlett stirred the paint extender powder with water. Jason had not seen this before. "Ms. Bartlett, that stuff you're mixing is yucky and gray. We can't paint with that." Jason looked closer at the paint

> extender. "Oh, it smells bad!"
>
> "Don't worry, Jason. We'll mix it with water and these pigments—different colors—and it will be fine. We won't make smelly paint."
>
> "Ms. Bartlett, I have a favor to ask."
>
> "Of course, Mrs. Jaines, how may I help you?"
>
> "We are having trouble getting Jason to try new foods at home. He'll eat macaroni and cheese, hotdogs, and toasted oat cereal. That's it. I make all of this wonderful food, and he's having none of it. What is he eating at school?"
>
> "We made homemade butter for science and baked Irish soda bread in our little oven. He was okay with the bread after he picked out all the raisins, and he loved the butter. You might think about having him help you cook. When he was involved with making the food, he showed more interest in eating it."
>
> "We can try that!"

Try one new food at a time in small portions repeatedly to increase children's acceptance. It may take ten or more exposures to the new food before it is accepted. Consider keeping different foods on the plate from touching. Some children become distressed when they find foods touching on their plates. Better to have the child mush foods closer by herself. It will save a food battle.

If a food is forbidden, children will express an increased preference for that food. Too much food on the plate may cause children to feel overwhelmed, then disinterested in eating. The statement "eat everything on your plate before you can have dessert" encourages overeating and implies that dessert is more important than the rest of the meal.

Healthy Snacks

Children eat what they see their friends and family eat. Offer small, healthy snacks during the day. The following suggestions are delicious and easy to prepare.

- Nut butter with fruit or celery. Almond butter is a good alternative to peanut butter.
- Crunchy veggies with ranch dressing. Hummus is a good alternative to ranch dressing.
- Brightly colored sliced bell peppers. Red, yellow, and orange peppers are sweeter than green ones.
- Mixed berries with a dollop of whipped cream.
- String cheese. Good protein source and fun to eat. How often do kids get to play with their food?
- Dip fruit pieces or graham crackers in yogurt. Two percent yogurt is good. Some fat is needed in the diet to absorb fat-soluble vitamins.
- Whole grain pretzels in sticks or traditional curves. Pretzels can be used to spell out words and nibbled into letters and shapes. Combine with cubes of cheese to make three-dimensional shapes and objects. Traditional curved whole grain pretzels can be difficult to locate. I found them online at www.vitacost.com.
- Scrambled eggs with cheese. This high-protein snack will keep children full longer. Besides, sometimes it's fun to have breakfast at odd times.

Children have a limited capacity for food and burn energy quickly due to active play. Extra snacks between meals help satisfy energy requirements.

- A good diet will help keep children healthy.
- A poor diet strains children's immune systems, making them more susceptible to illness (Berk, 2002).
- Stress hand washing before touching food to reduce illness.

Parenting... A Work in Progress

A balanced diet eaten in small meals throughout the day will ensure that children have enough energy to play and learn. Talk to your children about different foods. Look through cookbooks or food websites for interesting recipes. Bring your children to the grocery store and have them pick out ingredients needed for some meals made at home. Let them help you in the kitchen. Preparation will take longer and be messier, but you will be sharing invaluable experiences with your child. When children have at least partial ownership of mealtime, they are more likely to eat what is served.

Sleep Habits and Problems in Early Childhood

During sleep, the mind and body develop, and the body heals itself. Growth hormone is released by the pituitary gland during sleep. A well-rested child is a happier child, better able to learn and play.

Generally, two- and three-year-olds sleep between twelve to thirteen hours. Four- to six-year-old children need ten to eleven hours of sleep per day. Preschool-aged children, especially, often require a one- or two-hour nap. Nap time typically ends by kindergarten, although children may need quiet playtime or rest after school to recharge.

Bedtime Rituals and Other Strategies

Many children benefit from a bedtime ritual.

> "Papa, what are we reading tonight for our bedtime story?"
> "We're going to start *Mary Poppins* tonight, Laurel. Would you bring it to me? It's on top of the dresser."
> Laurel rushed to the dresser. In her hurry, she almost walked into her sister, Julia. "Laurel, watch out. You almost banged into me!"
> I peeked into the girls' bedroom. "Papa, the girls forgot to brush their teeth. Girls, get moving. Use that two-minute timer, and do a good job brushing. Make sure all those sugar bugs are brushed away."
> "Bugs? That's disgusting Mom," Laurel said as she walked into the bathroom.
> "Julia, move over. This has got to be the world's smallest sink."

> "No, you move over. I was here first."
> I stood in the bathroom doorway. "Ladies, stop arguing. The longer you take, the less time you have to read *Mary Poppins*. Now get a move on."

Difficulty falling asleep may result from some separation anxiety. Anxious children cannot sleep. Troubled sleep may also happen due to overstimulation just before bedtime in the form of physical activity or stimulating beverages. I made the mistake of giving my children some iced coffee within a few hours of bedtime. That mistake didn't happen twice.

A nightlight and an attachment object to shift from parent to toy may ease these feelings. Julia carried her Bonkie—an attachment object in the form of a blanket—nightly to help her sleep. Bonkie was a comfort she needed, aside from the bedtime ritual. Both Julia and Laurel used nightlights to keep away any monsters that might try to frighten them during the night. Ralph and I explained to the girls that anything bothering them in the night was not as powerful as the girls were themselves. All they needed to do was tell the monsters to go away, and the monsters had no choice but to listen.

Another strategy we used successfully was book therapy or bibliotherapy. Many books are available covering the topic of monsters in ways that make children feel more in control of their emotions. *Pog*, written by Lyn Lee and illustrated by Kim Gamble, is about a monster who is afraid of children. The local library has a list of bibliotherapy books that cover a wide range of topics including moving, illness, bullies, divorce, getting lost, manners, and more (Bibliotherapy, 2014).

Sleep is important for the growth and development of the body and brain. Dreaming is necessary to process the experiences of the day. Sufficient sleep enables the growth of children's intelligence, health, and well-being.

Explaining Death to Young Children

> Group time was already in session when a student and her mother entered the classroom. Mrs. Rozelle's eyes looked red-rimmed, her face blotchy from crying. Holly, her four year old daughter, put her belongings in a cubby and joined her classmates. The lead teacher, concerned with Mrs. Rozelle's state, asked her teaching assistant to continue reading a story to the students.
>
> Mrs. Rozelle stood by the cubbies, unable to move. She looked at her daughter with tenderness and grief. Seeing that something was desperately wrong, the preschool teacher asked Mrs. Rozelle to step out into the hallway.
>
> The teacher asked Mrs. Rozelle if there was anything she could do to help. Mrs. Rozelle looked towards the hallway floor and shook her head. There was nothing anyone could do.
>
> "Just a moment, let me ask the director to work with the students."
>
> The teacher stepped quietly into the classroom. "Jean, one of our parents needs assistance. Can you please help with group-time for a while?"
>
> The director looked up from her paperwork. "Of course, take all the time you need."
>
> Mrs. Rozelle had not moved from her spot in the hallway, still in her grief.
>
> The teacher asked, "May I hug you?" and held out her arms.

Mrs. Rozelle moved closer to receive a hug. She sobbed quietly on the teacher's shoulder. After a few moments, Mrs. Rozelle took a deep breath and stepped out of the embrace.

"Would you like to talk about it?" the teacher asked.

Mrs. Rozelle dug out some tissue from her purse and dabbed her eyes. "Two months ago, Holly's sister was diagnosed with an incurable disease. In order for her to have this particular illness, both parents had to carry the recessive gene. Unfortunately, both of us have it. We never thought to have genetic testing.

"We decided to have Holly tested, just in case. The doctors told us there was a one in four chance that Holly would have the disease. We were so hopeful, but . . ." Mrs. Rozelle began to cry again. "There are worse things than going blind. That's the first thing this horrible disease does to the children. Most don't live past adolescence. These are the only children I have. I'm losing them both." Mrs. Rozelle wiped her nose with the damp tissue.

"Here, let me get you some more tissue."

Mrs. Rozelle smiled for a fleeting moment. "No. I should get going. I have to talk with my older daughter's teacher. I'll come back for Holly when class is over."

The teacher watched Mrs. Rozelle turn to walk away. "Please let us know if there is anything we can do. We want to help."

Mrs. Rozelle stopped and turned towards the teacher. "Just continue to care for my baby. She enjoys coming to school and loves her teachers."

At the next staff meeting two days later, we discussed the situation with Holly's family. We decided to include death in our curriculum. Jean located a handbook for parents and teachers titled Young Children and Death by Dr. Jan Hare and Barbara Courier of the University of Wisconsin.

> After receiving approval from the parent board, the director and teachers began by talking about death of family pets. The following week during large group times, the preschool teachers asked the students if any of them had pets. The classmates made graphs of the different types and numbers of pets for math. The students dictated stories about pets.
>
> Late in the week, one of the students mentioned he used to have a dog, but the dog died and now lived in heaven. This statement opened the flood gates. The students, still learning to raise hands to take turns, tried to wait patiently for their turns to talk about their pets that died.
>
> The conversations turned to family members. The passings of grandmas, grandpas, aunts, and uncles were included in many conversations. Holly listened. She spoke of her dog, Rosie, who still lived. Holly never spoke of death. That was okay with her teachers. That Holly listened was enough.

During the preschool years, children do not see death as final. They have no concept of time and do not understand that death is irreversible. If a child is told that the person or pet is only sleeping, the child will believe the loved one will eventually wake up.

The only way to understand death is to talk about it. Children will have less anxiety about death if they are given an opportunity to discuss it. The adults in children's lives need to overcome their own anxieties regarding death so their children will not suffer similar feelings.

In order to understand the concept of death, children need to know what plants and animals need in order to live. When researchers asked four- to six-year-olds whether dead people use the bathroom, need food, air, or water, whether they sleep and dream, and whether a cut on their hand would heal, more than half answered yes (Slaughter et al., 1999).

Parenting... A Work in Progress

By age seven, most children understand death is final and eventually all living things die. In areas war-torn and bombarded by violence, children as young as five understand the concept of death (Mahon et al., 1999). Children understand what they experience.

> Seven-year-old Julia ran into the living-room, eyes shining with tears.
>
> "Something's wrong with Brownie. He's not moving!"
>
> All four of us went to the room that Julia shared with her sister and two gerbils, Brownie and Marshmallow.
>
> Marshmallow lay on top of Brownie, as if trying to keep him warm. Julia's dad, Ralph, reached into the gerbils' cage and picked up the tiny, unmoving gerbil.
>
> "Julia, Brownie is dead. I am so sorry. Would you like to hold him?"
>
> Julia nodded her head and held out her hands to hold her gerbil. She sat down on her bed, held Brownie closely, and stroked his soft brown fur.
>
> "Can we have a funeral for him?"
>
> "Of course," I replied, putting my arm around Julia.
>
> "I have a little box we could use for him if you want." Julia's sister, Laurel, put the box on top of Julia's bed.
>
> Julia, still stroking Brownie's fur, made an interesting request. "His favorite treat was sunflower seeds. We should put some in the box with him. Oh, and we could put his favorite sock in it, too."
>
> Ralph turned to me. "This is feeling rather Egyptian."
>
> I smiled and nodded.
>
> Julia put Brownie into the box along with his favorite seeds and sock. She carried her deceased pet out to the hill, under a pine tree. Ralph dug a hole large enough for Brownie's casket. After placing Brownie in the ground, we all took turns putting dirt on the burial site and said something special about Brownie. Julia

> went last.
>
> After the funeral ended Julia sat with me in the living room.
>
> "Brownie can't come back to us, but the part of him you loved best will live in your heart and in your memory," I said, "so, in a way, he is with you. It was just his body that died."

Brownie was the first in a long line of family pets to live with us and then pass from this existence, still loved by Julia and family. Acknowledging children's feelings and questions, even on topics uncomfortable for the adults in their lives, is paramount.

The following list of children's books (from the Carnegie Library of Pittsburg) deal with death and dying:

- *The Purple Balloon* by Chris Raschka.
- *I Miss You: A First Look at Death* by Pat Thomas, illustrated by Lesley Harker.
- *The Scar* by Charlotte Moundlic, illustrated by Olivier Tallec.
- *Water Bugs and Dragonflies: Explaining Death to Young Children* by Doris Stickney, illustrated by Robyn Henderson Nordstrom.
- *Goodbye Mousie* by Robie H. Harris, illustrated by Jan Ormerod.
- *When Dinosaurs Die: A Guide to Understanding Death* by Laurie Krasny, illustrated by Marc Brown.
- *Muddles, Puddles, and Sunshine: Your Activity Book to Help When Someone Has Died* by Diana Crossley, illustrated by Kate Sheppard.
- *The Bear and the Wildcat* by Kazumi Yumoto.
- *The Copper Tree: Helping a Child Cope with Death and Loss* by Hilary Robinson, illustrated by Mandy Stanley.
- *Help Me Say Goodbye: Activities for Helping Kids Cope when a Special Person Dies* by Janis Silverman.

References for Early Childhood

Berk, L. (2002). *Infants, children, and adolescents* (pp. 294-332). Boston, MA: Allyn and Bacon.

Bibliotherapy book lists. (2014). Helping young children cope in today's world. Pittsburg, PA: University of Pittsburg. Retrieved from http://www.carnegielibrary.org/research/parentseducators/parents/bibliotherapy/.

Chugani, H. T. (1994). Development of regional brain glucose metabolism in relation to behavior and plasticity. In G. Dawson & K. W. Fisher (Eds.), *Human behavior and the developing brain* (pp. 153-175). New York, NY: Guilford.

Copley, J. (2000). *The young child and mathematics*. New York, NY: National Association for the Education of Young Children.

Hare, J., & Courier, B. (1987). *Young children and death, a handbook for parents and teachers*. Menomonie, WI: University of Wisconsin.

Mahon, M. M., Goldberg, E. Z., & Washington, S. K. (1999). Concept of death in a sample of Israeli kibbutz children. *Death Studies, 23*, 43-59.

McGuinness, D. & Pribram, K. H. (1980). The neuropsychology of attention: Emotional and motivational controls. In M. C. Wittcock (Ed.), *The brain and psychology* (pp. 95-139). New York, NY: Academic Press.

Slaughter, V., Jaakkola, R., & Carrey, S. (1999). Constructing a coherent theory: Children's biological understanding of life and death. In M. Siegel & C. C. Peterson (Eds.), *Children's understanding of biology and health* (pp. 71-96). Cambridge, UK: Cambridge University Press.

Taylor, M., Cartwright, B. S., & Carlson, S. M. (1993). A developmental investigation of children's imaginary companions. *Developmental Psychology, 29*, 276-285.

Toma, John J. (07/2014 and 08/2014). Interviews, child development.

Early Childhood Further Reading

Anderson-McNamee, J. K., & Bailey, S. J. (04/2010). *The importance of play in early childhood development*. Retrieved from Montana State University Extension website: http://store.msuextension.org.

Chudler, E. H. (n.d.). *Neuroscience for kids: Do we use only 10% of our brains?* Retrieved from https://faculty.washington.edu/chudler/tenper.html.

Consultative Group on Early Childhood Care and Development. (n.d.). *Early childhood development from two to six years of age*. Retrieved from http://www.talkingpage.org/research.html

Lee, K. (2014). 5 year olds and social development: All about 5-year-olds' relationships with their social circle and beyond. *Parenting School-Age Children*. About.com. Retrieved from http://childparenting.about.com/od/socialdevelopment/a/Your-5-Year-Old-Child-5-Year-Old-Social-Development.htm.

Lee, L., & Gamble, K. (2002). *Pog*. Norwood, South Australia: Omnibus Books.

Nannis, E., & Cowen, P. (1987). Emotional understanding: A matter of age, dimension, and point of view. *Journal of Applied Developmental Psychology, 8*, 289-304.

Sachan, D. (2007). Behave yourself! Kids who can control their impulses do better in school. *Scientific American Mind, 18*(4), 11.

Technical Assistance & Training System. (01/2010). *Developmentally Appropriate Practice: Adaptive/Self-Help Skills*. Retrieved from http://tats.ucf.edu/docs/eUpdates/Curriculum-14.pdf

Toma, John J. Ph.D. Neuropsychology. Biltmore Evaluation and Treatment Services. Phoenix, Arizona.

Ways to Encourage Self-Help Skills in Children. (5/01/2012). *eXtension*. Retrieved from http://www.extension.org/pages/26436/ways-to-encourage-self-help-skills-in-children#.U1lhwFfAunx.

Parenting... A Work in Progress

Section 3

Middle Childhood— Ages Six through Twelve

The brain reaches 95 percent of its adult size by age six, while the rest of the body grows at a slower rate, allowing school-aged children to use their brain power to learn before becoming physically mature.

Middle childhood-aged children hop, skip, throw, and jump. They can coordinate movements of various body parts, enabling them to participate in sports. Their ability to print, write in cursive letters, and perceive depth improves dramatically during middle childhood.

During middle childhood, spanning ages six to eleven, children blend social conventions into their definitions of who they believe they are. These feelings happen without an adult pointing out shortcomings and accomplishments. Seven- to eight-year-olds believe feelings are hidden away because they are inside a person (Nannis & Cowan, 1987). They feel pride and shame. "By age 8, children understand they can experience more than one emotion at a time" (Berk, 2002, p. 490).

The school-aged child's brain responds to a call to trim back about half of the connections within his or her brain. As discussed earlier, this process is referred to as synaptic pruning. Think of a tree that has too many small branches that need reshaping, strengthening. Prune off what is unnecessary. This is similar to what is happening within the brain of your child. By age eight, the brain is fully developed physically. The prefrontal cortex is shaping and preparing to incorporate new experiences (Toma, 2014). School-aged children begin to think abstractly around age eight.

The heavy synaptic pruning that happens in pre-adolescence helps the brain transition from childhood to adulthood. Learning is easier in childhood, but the adult brain can focus longer on a single problem and carry out more complex thought processes (Moskowitz, 2009).

As children enter middle childhood, ideas of fairness are based on equality. Everyone gets the same share of the treasure, unlike early childhood, when everything is "*mine* unless it is broken. Then it's *yours*." Around age seven, children believe if they work extra hard, they should get more. By eight, children reason that special consideration should be given to those in need. Advice and support from parents can help develop this sense of justice, but the give and take of peer interaction is vitally important.

Typically developing children who experience love will be more likely to become loving individuals. Those who are ignored will find it difficult to love themselves or others. Parents who model love and friendship encourage their children to do the same. Parents cannot choose their children's friends but can instill within their family the security of love, which will help children attain the high self-esteem needed to remain emotionally balanced and capable of good judgment.

Physical Development in Middle Childhood

Body development is ingenious in design. The brain reaches 95 percent of adult size by age six while the rest of the body grows at a slower rate. The difference in brain-body growth allows school-aged children to use their brain power to learn before attaining physical maturity.

Middle childhood-aged children hop, skip, throw, and jump. They know how to coordinate movements of various body parts, enabling them to participate in sports. The ability to print, write in cursive letters, and develop an understanding of depth improves dramatically during middle childhood.

"What happened to you?"

Your child's brain is responding to a call to trim back about 50% of the connections within his or her brain. The prefrontal cortex is shaping and preparing to incorporate new experiences (Toma, 2014). It happens to everyone.

> Alma and George stared at each other, jaws open wide—stunned. "What happened to our understanding child? Adam has always been so empathetic!" George turned and gave Adam, his eleven year old son, a withering glance.
> Adam rolled his eyes, "What? All I said to Grandma was the pajamas she gave me were lame."

Adam's reaction to his parent's disbelief was confusion. Adam believed that he spoke his true feelings to his Grandmother. Not long ago, he would have thanked her with a smile, keeping his thoughts to himself. Adam loved his Grandma and wanted her to be happy.

Preteen and teens have difficulty reading facial emotions, often mistaking other's feelings—making them seem callous at times.

A large head does not necessarily mean great intelligence. According to a 1999 study by a research team at the Faculty of Health Sciences at McMaster University, Albert Einstein's brain was *smaller* than average, but some areas of his brain were larger—specifically the areas linked to mathematical ability and visuospatial cognition. These areas are associated with the ability to creatively make unusual associations, allowing him to think about time and space as he did. (Grinnell, 2012)

Obesity and Malnutrition

Early malnutrition, a devastating issue for developing nations, may cause the brain structures responsible for appetite control to be set at a higher setting (Barker, 1994; Popkin, 1994) and interfere with intellectual performance throughout life (Scrimshaw, 1997). The higher setting causes the body to allow a later than normal "stop eating" signal, fooling the body so it consumes more food than necessary. This is different from when the mouth wants more but the body isn't hungry.

If the body senses it is starving, it protects itself by slowing its metabolic rate to stretch energy resources. Slower metabolic rate puts children at risk for obesity, along with heart problems, emotional issues, and the social issues that follow.

In developed countries such as the United States, food is plentiful, but quick and easy "junk" food contributes poor nutrients to the body. "For each additional hour of TV watched on weekends at age 5, the risk of adult obesity increased by 7%" (Viner & Cole, 2005).

"The marketing of food and non-alcoholic beverages to children is very potent and highly influential (Cairns et al., 2009). Particularly strong evidence exists that links television advertising to children's food knowledge, preferences, purchase requests, and consumption patterns. Furthermore, television advertising is associated with increased consumption of snacks and drinks high in sugar, as well as excess calorie intake" (WHO, 2011; *Population-based approaches to CHILDHOOD OBESITY PREVENTION*, World Health Organization, p. 28).

> The family watched television while they ate dinner in the living room. When the food was finished, they waited for a commercial break to clean up the dishes. Mom scooped up the leftovers, walked in the kitchen, and said, "Pause the program so we can fast forward through the commercials. I don't like commercials."
>
> Timmy helped his mother pick up some of the plates and followed her. "Mom, how come you don't like commercials?"
>
> "Those commercials make me want to buy things I don't need, especially the one with the double chocolate caramel brownie. You know, the one with ice cream covered with chocolate and caramel sauces. I'm not hungry, but I want it anyway. Besides, I'm trying to be a role model for your older brother."
>
> "I hear you, Mom. Those idiots at school call him Buddha-Belly Bill. That's not cool."

Obesity carries with it serious health consequences. "Raised body mass index (BMI) is a major risk factor for diseases such as cardiovascular disease, type 2 diabetes and many cancers including, colorectal cancer, kidney cancer and esophageal cancer. . . . (Ezzati et al., 2004; World Cancer Research Fund, 2007). Overweight and obesity in children are associated with significant reductions in quality of life (Tsiros et al., 2009; Williams et al., 2005) and a greater risk of teasing, bullying and social isolation" (Lobstein et al., 2004; Population-based approaches to CHILDHOOD OBESITY PREVENTION, World Health Organization, p. 13).

The best way to help is to change family behavior. One person cannot have an effective life change and be tortured daily by seeing the rest of the family eat whatever they want, whenever they wish. For

Parenting... A Work in Progress

long-lasting, positive results, every member of the family must partake in the lifestyle change. It is a long-lasting, lifesaving family activity.

Other Screen-Time Statistics

According to the Henry J. Kaiser Foundation, children eight to eighteen spend the following amount of time in front of some type of screen each day:
- Approximately 7.5 hours using entertainment media.
- Approximately 4.5 hours watching TV.
- Approximately 1.5 hours on the computer.
- More than an hour playing video games.

In stark contrast, children spend just **25 minutes per day** reading books.

Suggestions:
- Have frequent family meals without the presence of media. Watching the screen during meals does not encourage the conversations that are needed to promote good family relationships.
- Build leisure time into meals. Eating while relaxed allows for better digestion.
- Slow the rate of food consumption. Eating slowly gives the stomach time to realize it is full. The stomach tells the brain when it doesn't need any more food. If a person eats too quickly, the stomach doesn't have enough time to tell the brain "no more, thank you," and the individual ends up feeling overfull.
- Consider a thirty-minute walk after dinner. Explore the neighborhood. Let go of some stress. Walking improves digestion and helps you sleep better. Call it the evening constitutional.

> After my mother-in-law no longer had the energy to entertain large holiday meals, I chose to take on the Buikema Thanksgiving dinner. The first year I did this, I noticed most of the participants went into a "food coma" after dinner. I was happy the meal went over well, but falling asleep right after eating is never a good thing.
>
> The following year, I suggested we all go for a walk after dinner in the guise of having more room later for dessert. Not everyone was interested, but most did venture outside for an after-dinner stroll around the neighborhood. When we returned, those who chose to go on the walk didn't feel the need for an after-dinner nap.

- Use a favorite activity for positive reinforcement instead of food. If food is the reward for a job well done, eating will be associated with parental acceptance. "Eat, be happy" is not the best outcome.
- Be patient. If weight loss is a goal, remember that all the weight did not show up in one day. It accumulated over time. Stressing over pounds will only make it more difficult to lose them.

Parenting... A Work in Progress

Self-Esteem in Middle Childhood

Preteen Emotions

When children begin school, they receive feedback about their performance as compared to their schoolmates. The children's self-esteem adjusts accordingly.

"By age 7 to 8 children have formed at least four separate types of self-esteem: academic, social, athletic, and appearance. Physical appearance weighs in heaviest in determining self-esteem" (Berk, 2002, p. 484). Society's emphasis on appearance influences children's acceptance of themselves.

During middle childhood, ages six to eleven, children weave social conventions into their definitions of who they believe they are. These feelings happen without an adult pointing out shortcomings and accomplishments. They feel pride and shame. "By age 8, children understand they can experience more than one emotion at a time" (Berk, 2002, p. 490).

> "Look, Gordie, there's a present for you from Grandma!"
>
> Gordie hesitated a moment before ripping off the wrapping paper covered in glittery Santa bunnies. He tried to smile. "Oh, bunny slippers! That's nice." Gordie turned toward his older brother who sat next to him squelching a laugh. As quietly as he could, Gordie said to his brother, "You'd think Grandma would remember I'm eleven."
>
> Gordie felt happy his grandmother sent him a

> present, but he was disappointed that it was bunny slippers. Gordie loved his grandma. He would thank her when he saw her to make her feel happy. He has become better at masking his emotions.

Preteens realize their parents don't know everything. These children feel they are smarter than their parents. Hormonal changes during puberty affect feelings and judgment, causing emotional pain to feel stronger. Between the hormonal madness of puberty and a tendency toward self-centeredness, their behavior towards parents may run from being aloof to serious rejection. They are afraid of fitting in and seem hypercritical and overly sensitive. Filled with anxiety and doubt, self esteem may plummet.

Developmental Delays

Children with developmental delays, sensitivity issues, and attention deficits have all the same emotional issues compounded by the symptoms of their disability.

According to the Center for Disease Control and Prevention (CDC), a national health interview survey taken in 2012 states the number of children three to seventeen years of age ever diagnosed with ADHD is 5.9 million. However, there is no one test to diagnose ADHD, and problems like depression, anxiety, and some learning disabilities can display similar symptoms (cdc.gov, 2014).

In children with ADHD, the brain matures in a normal pattern, but in some areas development is delayed by three years compared to children who do not have ADHD. Areas of the frontal cortex, responsible for the ability to suppress inappropriate actions and thoughts, focus attention, remember things from moment to moment, work for reward, and control movement, mature later than those of children without ADHD. The area of the brain that does mature faster is the motor cortex, which may explain the restlessness and fidgety symptoms typical in hyperactive children (NIMH Child Psychiatry Branch, 2007).

People with attention deficit disorder with hyperactivity tend to have "reduced electrical flow activity in the frontal lobe and cerebral cortex and in other areas responsible for attention and inhibition of behavior" (Berk, 2002, p. 446). Parents may decide, with the support of their physician, to use medication. Drugs used for attention deficit disorder with and without hyperactivity are more effective when used in combination with counseling.

How Schools Can Help

> Carlos, a highly intelligent, creative, fourth-grade student, couldn't sit still in school and was unable to read the board. Discovering a need for glasses improved his schoolwork, but the constant moving around in his seat distracted his teacher. "Carlos, sit still."
>
> "I'm trying to, Teacher."
>
> "Try harder. You are distracting your classmates."
>
> "Yes, Teacher."
>
> Carlos's teacher called his parents to ask if he had difficulty sitting still at home. "Yes, he always moves around. Even when he watches TV, he only sits still for a few minutes. He likes to do several things at once. Carlos is just like his uncle, always moving."
>
> Carlos' teacher spoke with the special education teacher at school. After describing what happened in the classroom and at home, they developed a plan. The plan was revised with the input of Carlos and his parents and put into effect the following week.
>
> The plan involved changing everyone's desk from rows to groups of four. This allowed for more physical movement during the day; students could change groups for different subjects. Carlos' desk was toward the back of the room. When he needed to, he was allowed to stand up and work. Sometimes he paced quietly in the back of the room. Carlos needed to move around in order to think. Sometimes it appeared he was not paying

> attention, but when asked questions, he answered them correctly. Carlos heard and understood everything.
>
> The new arrangement did not cause Carlos to be any less hyperactive, but it did change his academic status and sense of success. Carlos was given some control over his environment. The groupings benefited the entire class. It allowed for more varied social interaction and happier students.

All children are unique in ability and personality. The belief that the same teaching methods will work for all is like saying the same medication will work for everyone. Neither is true.

Look for these elements in your school system. If not available, consider bringing the following suggestions to the attention of the local school board, as they may be beneficial:

- Frequent breaks during the day. Students need time to get the wiggles out. Concentration is improved when time to play and run is given throughout the day.
- A longer school day to make certain no subject matter is shorted. The arts are not extra. They are part of the culture.
- A longer school year. The United States does not have an agrarian society anymore. The majority of children are not harvesting crops.
- Center-based classrooms. Students work individually or in small groups on specific learning tasks. Examples are computer center, math center, reading center, science center.
- Frequent, positive, parent–teacher communication. Mutual respect is key.

When families, schools, and society work cooperatively, a superior educational system may be constructed. Our future depends upon the importance we place on our children.

Parenting... A Work in Progress

Fairness, Friendship, and Love in Middle Childhood

Suggestions to Improve Peer Relations

Fairness doesn't mean everyone gets the same thing. It means all get what they need—a tough lesson to learn.

As children enter middle childhood, ideas of fairness are based on equality. Everyone gets the same share of the treasure, unlike early childhood when everything is "mine unless it is broken. Then it's yours." Around age seven children see fairness in terms of merit. If you work extra hard, you should get more. By eight, children reason that special consideration should be given to those in need. Parental advice and support can help develop this sense of justice, but the give and take of peer interaction is vitally important (Dunn, 1996; Hartup, 1983; Parker & Asher, 1987).

Aggression lessens in middle childhood, but verbal insults abound, especially among boys. Girls tend to use social exclusion. Peer groups are formed, and the social shuffle begins. Within the groups, children find roles to play. There are leaders, followers, cooperation within the group, and a sense of loyalty to these friends.

Peer acceptance—likability—is a strong predictor of current as well as later psychological adjustment. Those children who are rejected by their peers often have difficulty knowing what to do in social situations. Some interventions to improve peer relations are:

- Model how to enter a group. Some children walk right in and start talking immediately on a topic not related to the group discussion.

- Practice interacting with a peer. Conversation is an art form that requires practice.
- Show what cooperation in play looks like. The ability to be a good loser or winner is important for acceptance.
- Model how to respond to another child with friendly emotion and approval.
- Tutor academics if needed. Low grades equal frustration, which may lead to poor peer relations.
- Practice games played in school. Few things hurt as much as always being the last picked.

Let's Be Friends

During early childhood, a friend was someone who played with the same kinds of toys and was physically nearby. In middle childhood, friendship transitions from someone who does what you want them to do to being mutually helpful. The focus is still self-interest. Once a friendship is formed, trust is the most important element. Many friendships last for several years.

"By age 8 or 9, children have just a handful of people they call friends, often only one best friend… Children like to choose friends that are similar to themselves in personality, achievements, age, sex, race, ethnicity, and social economic status… Schools and neighborhoods influence the choices of friends. In integrated schools, as many as half the students reported close friendships with other race-friends" (Berk, 2002, p. 497).

Children learn the importance of commitment through friendships. They learn it is possible to argue, resolve conflicts, and remain friends.

Not all friends are good for pro-social development. Aggressive friendships between children may lead to antisocial behavior. While most children tend to avoid their overly aggressive peers, some appear to be drawn to them like a moth to a flame.

Karen and Alicia lived a few houses apart and were in the same third grade classroom. Alicia, a quiet child, wished she were bold like Karen, who did whatever she wanted. No one bothered Karen. "Come on, Alicia. I want to get some candy at the corner store."

"I don't have any money, Karen. I can't buy anything."

"Don't worry, Ali. Let's go." The girls walked three blocks to the store. Karen opened the door, looked left, then right, and walked inside. Alicia followed closely behind her. "Hey, Karen, I thought you were going to buy some candy. It's right over there by the register."

"Not so loud. I never said anything about buying. I said I want to get some candy. Now when I say go, grab what you want and walk out the door. If you run, they'll know you did something."

"No way! That's stealing. I don't want to get in trouble. I'll get caught for sure, and my parents will ground me forever!"

"You worry too much. Look, watch me." Karen waited until no one was looking, took a candy bar off the shelf, and slipped it into her pocket. "See how easy that was? Now you do it."

Alicia wanted her new friend's approval, so she grabbed a candy bar and both girls walked out of the store.

"I told you it'd be easy. See?" Karen ripped open her candy as they walked back towards their neighborhood. "Why didn't you open yours?"

"I'm not very hungry. I'll eat it later."

Alicia felt guilty. She couldn't eat stolen candy, and she didn't want Karen to be mad at her or think she was a baby.

"I have to go home. My stomach hurts. See ya tomorrow, Karen." Alicia walked towards her home, cut through a neighbor's yard, and hurried back to

> the corner store. When no one was looking, she put the candy bar on top of the counter. As she turned to leave, the clerk noticed Alicia and asked if she wanted anything. "No, thanks. I changed my mind."

If a friendship becomes a source of stress, it's time for parents to take action. Parents might start by talking to their child and encouraging him to share his feelings with the friend. Adults should also help children understand the importance of walking away from the situation, especially if the friend is being physically or emotionally hurtful. Parents and other adults can try to establish some distance between the child and the friend.

Love Is in the Air

From a biological basis, when people fall in love, the brain releases chemicals that stimulate the brain's pleasure center. Later, the relationship endures with attachment based on shared interests. I like to look at love as the willingness to give of the self unconditionally.

During middle childhood, children are learning to deal with fear and pleasure in a social context. Dealing with these two basic emotions is difficult.

Love can be confusing at any age. During middle childhood boys and girls show their liking for one another in distinctly different ways.

> **Girl's View**
>
> "Dad, the strangest thing happened today."
> "What's going on, Georgia?"
> "Well, you know Tommy from school, right? Today he walked up to me, punched me on the arm, smiled really big, and told me I was a big fat slob. What's wrong with him!?"
> Georgia's father put his arm around her. "Honey, he's trying to tell you he likes you."
> "What? You're kidding, right? That's stupid."
> "That's exactly right, Georgia. Boys are stupid,

especially when it comes to talking to girls. Sorry, honey. They get smarter eventually."

Boy's View

When David came home from school, sat down, and stared at the kitchen wall with confusion written on his face, his mother knew something was wrong. He muttered to himself, and shook his head.

"At school, this girl gave me a folded up piece of paper. You'll never believe what it said."

David's mother sat down on one of the other kitchen chairs. "Tell me, oh handsome one. What did it say?"

"Cut it out, Ma. It's not my fault the girls in my class keep calling. Anyway, I open it up and it says 'Do you like me? Check this box.' Then it had a box next to yes, maybe, and no."

"What did you do?"

"I checked maybe and gave it back to her. I don't know. It was so weird!"

David's mother raised his chin in her hand and smiled. "David, just be your regular, easy-going self and try not to worry about it. She's just being a normal girl."

Love Defined

In an unattributed survey, elementary school-aged children were asked "What is love?" The answers from their young and innocent minds were surprising.

- "Love is when my sister fixes my hair every day."
  —Valerie, age five
- "When my grandmother got arthritis, she couldn't bend over and paint her toenails anymore. So my grandfather does it for her all the time, even when his hands got arthritis too. That's love."
  —Rebecca, age eight
- "Love is when a girl puts on perfume and a boy puts on shaving cologne and they go out and smell each other." —Karl, age five

Middle Childhood—Ages Six through Twelve

- "Love is when you go out to eat and give somebody most of your French fries without making them give you any of theirs."
  —Chrissy, age six
- "Love is when my daddy makes me breakfast every morning."
  —Ian, age seven
- "Love is when you come to school and look at her all day."
  —Raul, age ten
- "Love is when you kiss all the time. Then when you get tired of kissing, you still want to be together and you talk more. My mommy and daddy are like that. They look gross when they kiss." —Emily, age eight
- "Love is when my daddy gives me the best piece of chicken."
  —Elaine, age five
- "Love is what's in the room with you at Christmas if you stop opening presents and look around." —Bobby, age seven
- "You really shouldn't say 'I love you' unless you mean it. But if you mean it, you should say it a lot. People forget." —Jessica, age eight

Build a Better Mattress

Think of the support system for the emotional self as a mattress. If situations push a person down, and the mattress is thick, built by the love and encouragement of the parents or other important adults in life, bouncing back from adversity is not as difficult. A thin mattress, built with little interest from parents or important adults, makes it difficult. The emotional turmoil will be hard to get over.

Children who experience love will be loving individuals. Those who are ignored will find it difficult to love themselves or others. Parents who model love and friendship encourage their children to do the same. Parents cannot choose their children's friends but can instill within their family the security of love, which will help children attain the high self-esteem needed to remain emotionally balanced and capable of good judgment.

Parenting Styles in Middle Childhood

"I'm doing the best I can. You didn't come with an instruction book!" (Source unknown)

Four Parenting Styles

There are four basic styles of parenting, according to psychologist Diana Baumrind's research. They are: authoritative, authoritarian, permissive, and uninvolved.

- **Authoritative**: Parents are attentive, forgiving, help their children know and understand desired behavior, have rules and structure, and explain the rules and the reasons behind them. If a child fails to follow the rules, the consequences are reasonable and expected. If rules are followed, reward/reinforcement follows. This parenting type includes give-and-take and negotiations between parents and children.
- **Authoritarian:** A strict parenting style, parent expectations are high, but limited communication takes place between child and parents. Parents don't provide logical reasoning for rules and limits and use a "my way or the highway, do as I say not as I do" attitude. Parents are prone to dole out harsh punishments.
- **Permissive:** Parents take on the role of "friends" rather than adult caregivers. They have few expectations of their child. These parents allow their children to make their own decisions. The children are forced to be their own parents.
- **Uninvolved**: Parents put their own lives before the child's. They provide for basic needs but show little interaction with the child (Baumrind, 1967; 1973).

Middle Childhood—Ages Six through Twelve

An eleven-year-old girl in fifth grade has been invited to a sleepover birthday party for one of her friends from school. All the students in class have been invited, boys as well as girls. The girls are good friends, but the parents do not know each other well. What to do?

Authoritative Perspective

Authoritative parents would explain the rules. If the parents are uncomfortable with the idea of their daughter spending the night in a situation such as this, the parents might say why this is not a good idea and develop a compromise with their child. These parents might call to confirm parental chaperoning, letting their daughter know she may attend the party even though she will not be staying overnight.

If the parents speak to the parents of the birthday girl and decide that suitable chaperoning and sleeping arrangements have been made, their daughter may attend the party for its full duration. If she should feel uncomfortable, she may call them up at any hour and she will be picked up and taken home. Their daughter will feel trusted.

Authoritarian Perspective

Authoritarian parents are strict without explaining their thought processes. These parents might disallow a continuation of friendship between the girls, as it may appear that the birthday girl's parents seem overly permissive. There is no room for compromise. This causes friction and resentment.

Permissive Perspective

Permissive parents may feel uncomfortable with the idea of a mixed group sleepover. Since they want a friendship rather than a guidance relationship with their children, they will allow their daughter to do as she pleases. These parents may be anxious but feel unable to do anything about it without endangering the friendly relationship with their child. Their daughter will have to make decisions, unguided.

Uninvolved Perspective

Uninvolved parents are not interested in the comings or goings of their children. No guidance is provided. She can attend or not. They do not care.

The following vignettes illustrate a child's experience from the four different parenting styles.

Authoritative parents develop a sense of mutual respect with their children. It takes a great deal of thought and effort. Parents need to think through what rules are important and show by action what it means to be a reasonable, humane person. This parenting style "produces children with high levels of self-reliance and self-esteem, who are socially responsible, independent and achievement-oriented" (Greenwood, 2014).

Consequences follow our actions. Consider the following scene.

> Suzie walked down the driveway on the way to her friend's house. She looked up as she heard a cat yowling from the roof of the next door neighbor's garage. The new skateboard, which she promised to put away after she finish playing, lay directly in her path. Suzie tripped over the skateboard and scraped her knee.
>
> "Ouch! Darn it, that smarts!" she hissed, as she rubbed her injured knee. "I better put this away before anyone else falls over this thing."
>
> Suzie's mom saw the action play itself out from the living room window. She opened up the garage door and walked outside to check on Suzie. There was blood oozing from Suzie's knee.
>
> The scrape and bleeding were natural consequence of Suzie's leaving her skateboard out. Suzie's mom stated the following:
>
> "Now look what happened to your knee! If you had put that rolling, miniature surfboard away right when you were finished playing with it, you wouldn't be all scraped up and bleeding. Go on now. Put that

skateboard away and get yourself cleaned up. I don't know what your grandpa was thinking, getting you that contraption."

Taken as a logical consequence through Authoritative parenting, the scene continues:

Suzie's mom followed her daughter into the house. Suzie leaned over her knee, careful to dab off the excess blood, and cleaned the scrape. Her mom handed her a towel to dry the wound.

"Here, take this bandage."

Suzie, sitting on a kitchen chair, winced as she placed the bandage on her knee. "Thanks, Mom. I've got to go. I was on my way to Liam's house when I fell over my skateboard."

"Hold on there, missy. What did your father and I say about leaving things out and not putting them away? We just talked about this today during breakfast."

Holding her chin up on her palm, elbow firmly placed on the kitchen table, Suzie said nothing.

Suzie's mom pulled a kitchen chair close to her daughter's. "What's the rule?"

"You said I had to put away my belongings when I finished using them, or else they would be yours for two days. Do you really have to take my skateboard away? Please don't, Momma!"

"Suzie, you know I love you, right?"

Her daughter nodded and looked at the kitchen floor.

"Your father and I make rules to help keep you safe. We all came up with this rule together. Everyone agreed. Now, if you'd put the skateboard away, would you be sitting here all banged up, or would you be at Liam's house, having fun with your friends?"

Suzie took a huge breath through her nose. "Yes, Momma, I agreed. I know. I'll remember for next time. Can I go now?"

Parenting... A Work in Progress

> "Yes, Suz, you can go. Be back in time for dinner."
> Suzie stood up and gave her mom a hug. "Okay, Momma. I'll see you later."

Logical consequences, planned in advance with a discussion of the reasons for their need, help the child to learn internal control. Suzie, having lost the opportunity to play with her new skateboard for two days, will be more likely to put it away next time. Not only does she want to keep it, she realized if the skateboard is left out someone else might get hurt or her board may be stolen.

The same scenario, taken from a perspective of Authoritarian parenting:

> "Here, take this bandage."
> Suzie, sitting on a kitchen chair, winced as she placed the bandage on her knee. "Thanks, Mom. I've got to go. I was on my way to Liam's house when I fell over my skateboard."
> "I don't think so, young lady. Go to your room right now."
> Suzie stared at her mom. "But Momma . . ."
> "Don't 'but Momma' me! Get to your room, now. What if your grandpa fell over that thing? Just you wait 'til your father comes home. You're in for a spanking."
> Head down, Suzie walked up stairs and shut her bedroom door. She sat on her bed and cried.

Suzie lost the opportunity to use her skateboard, her free time lost to the long wait for Dad to come home and punish her. Suzie learned anxiety and fear come from making a mistake.

The scenario, taken from a perspective of Permissive parenting:

> "Here, take this bandage."
> Suzie, sitting on a kitchen chair, winced as she placed the bandage on her knee. "Thanks, Mom. I've

> got to go. I was on my way to Liam's house when I fell over my skateboard."
>
> "Okay, Suzie-Q, have fun at Liam's. Say hi to his mom for me."
>
> Suzie looked at her mother with disdain. "Mom, don't call me that. I hate that name. It makes me sound like some kind of dessert." Suzie stormed out the kitchen.
>
> Mother, embarrassed, called after her daughter as she closed the door to leave for Liam's. "Sorry, dear."

Suzie treated her mother as a peer. Mother had not parented her daughter. There were no rules. Suzie said and did as she pleased.

The same scenario, taken from a perspective of Uninvolved parenting:

> "Here, take this bandage."
>
> Suzie, sitting on a kitchen chair, winced as she placed the bandage on her knee. "Thanks Mom. I've got to go. I was on my way to Liam's house when I fell over my skateboard."
>
> "Well, be more careful next time. Someone might get hurt and sue me." Suzie's mother picked up the skateboard by one of the rear wheels. "I should really throw this thing out. What was your grandfather thinking, giving you this rolling lawsuit-in-the-making?" Mother handed the skateboard to Suzie. "Here, take this and put it in the garage. I'm going out. There are some frozen dinners in the refrigerator. Eat, if you feel like it."

Suzie was left to fend for herself. Her basic needs were met, but there was no feeling of family. Suzie was left to float on a cloud of parental uncertainty.

Parenting... A Work in Progress

Consequences help children learn from their mistakes. When parents use a firm, but respectful, approach to deal with the behavior, they can use logical consequences to discipline their children with great effectiveness. Punishment often erupts from anger and usually doesn't require much time and thought.

In the first scenario with authoritative parenting, Suzie had the opportunity to learn that, if she acted in a certain manner, she would be responsible for a known consequence. In the other scenarios, Suzie did not learn internal control. In the case of authoritarian parenting in particular, Suzie learned that adults get away with being bullies or intimidating the weak.

Punishment often causes children to focus their anger on their parents instead of learning to behave better. Instead of "I made a mistake," the child may think, "My mom is mean." Consequences allow children to learn from their mistakes and make better decisions in the future.

Not all parents have the same idea of best parenting practice. Whenever possible, be a united front to avoid children using, "But Mom said . . . But Dad said . . ." to get their way.

Home Alone in Middle Childhood

If time home alone cannot be avoided, make sure the child knows she may call the parent. Also have a neighbor check in on the kids, or be someone to go to if help is needed. Knowing someone trustworthy is nearby may alleviate the children's fear of being home without adults. Normal house noises always seem creepier when the authority figures aren't present.

Sometimes neighbors are not available, and relatives live far away. Maybe the family has recently moved to a new area and hasn't found after school care. In this case, the kids may need to be home alone.

Home Alone Ages by State

Although the National SAFEKIDS Campaign recommends that no child under the age of twelve be left at home alone, not all states have a minimum age listed for home-alone children.

According to Database Systems Corporation (latchkey-kids.com, 2014), the following states have no minimum age for home-alone children listed: Alabama, Arizona, Arkansas, Connecticut, Hawaii, Idaho, Iowa, Indiana, Louisiana, Maine, Massachusetts, Minnesota, Mississippi, Missouri, Montana, Nebraska, New Hampshire, New Jersey, New Mexico, New York, Ohio, Oklahoma, Pennsylvania, South Dakota, Texas, Utah, Virginia, Vermont, and Wyoming.

The following states are listed as unknown—no resources found: Alaska, California, Kentucky, Nevada, Rhode Island, South Carolina, Vermont, and West Virginia. These states expect parents to determine whether their children are mature enough to stay home alone. No specific age has been recommended or specified.

The minimum age recommendation for child home alone in Colorado is twelve, Delaware is twelve, Florida is eighteen, Georgia is eight, Kansas is twelve, Michigan is eleven, North Dakota is nine, Tennessee is ten, and Washington is ten.

The minimum age specified for child home alone in Illinois is fourteen, Maryland is eight, North Carolina is eight, and Oregon is ten.

"City and county ordinances within each state may have more definitive and restrictive laws. Call your State DHS or local child welfare agency to learn about age guidelines in your area." (Database Systems Corporation, 2014, latchkey-kids.com/latchkey-kids-age-limits)

When children are not supervised, it may be considered neglect, which falls under the category of child abuse. If you need help reaching the local child protective services agency, call Childhelp National Child Abuse Hotline at 800-4-A-CHILD (800-422-4453). Find more information on their website: www.childhelp.org.

> For one hour each day after school, sisters Amy, eleven, and Maria, nine, were to be home alone until their mom came home from work. The first two weeks went well. On Thursday of the third week, their dad noticed a mark on the wall just above the living room couch. "Girls, come over here for a minute." Both Amy and Maria walked into the living room. "What is that? Looks like a dent in the wall. Any idea what happened?"
>
> Knowing that telling the truth got them in less trouble, Amy fessed up. "Dad, we were having a backpack throwing contest."
>
> "Really! How did this work?"
>
> "You swing the backpack and throw it as far as you can," Maria said. "If your backpack goes the farthest, you win!"
>
> "Well, girls, nobody won this time. You told me the truth, so no one is in trouble. Now help me move the sofa. I need both of you to clean the scuff marks off the wall. Then I'll show you how to use spackle to fill that

> dent. Thankfully it's not too deep. You girls know this wasn't a smart thing to do, right? No more of this."
>
> Dad called out to Mom from the living room. "Hey Mom, our girls invented a fun new game."
>
> Mom looked at the dent. "Looks like we need to revisit the after-school program."

The Home Alone Quiz – Is Your Child Ready?

Source: singleparents.about.com/library/quiz/bl_home_alone_quiz
(Note: If it is not legal in the state in which you reside, your child may not stay home alone, even if you were able to answer "yes" to nineteen of the following twenty questions.)

1. Has your child demonstrated in multiple settings that he is consistently responsible (for example, at home, at school, and when visiting other friends' homes)?
2. Are the house rules, neighbors' phone numbers, your emergency contact information, and instructions for handling an emergency clearly posted in your home?
3. Is it legal in your state for your child to stay home alone?
4. Can your child explain to you in detail what she would do in an emergency, including a fire, an intruder, or a medical emergency?
5. Does your child know your home phone number and address?
6. Have you discussed with your child what kinds of situations require a call to 911?
7. Are there one or two neighbors nearby whom your child could call if he or she needed immediate assistance, but the emergency was not severe enough to warrant calling 911?
8. Does your child know what rules she must follow when you are not home?
9. Have you spoken with your child about what is expected of him while you are not home?
10. Has your child demonstrated that she can call you on your cell phone?

11. Does your child regularly follow your instructions even if you are not present?
12. Is your home childproof? (For example, are medicines and firearms locked up?)
13. Does your child know about the specific consequences that would apply if he chose not follow the rules while was home alone?
14. When using a cell phone to call 911, calls can sometimes be routed to regional call centers rather than local 911 operators. In this situation, the caller must be prepared to state her city and general type of emergency before being connected with local authorities. Would your child know how to do this if she had to call 911 from a cell phone?
15. Have you developed a routine for what your child will be doing while he is home alone?
16. Have you role played how to handle various emergency situations?
17. Is your child capable of calling 911 in an emergency, calmly explaining the problem, and stating your address?
18. Has your child told you explicitly that she feels confident to stay home alone?
19. Have you worked out a system for storing your front door key, either with your child or in a lock box outside your home?
20. Has your child demonstrated an ability to stand up to peer pressure and think for himself?

Home Alone Tips for Parents

Childwelfare.gov suggests the following tips for parents:
- Have a trial period. Leave the child home alone for a short time while staying close to home. See how she manages.
- Role play. Act out possible situations to help your child learn what to do, such as how to manage visitors who come to the door or how to answer phone calls so the caller doesn't know parents are not home.

- Establish rules. Make sure your child knows what is and is not allowed when you are not home. Set clear limits on the use of television, computers and other electronic devices, and the Internet.
- Have a list of chores other tasks to keep children busy while parents are gone.
- Discuss emergencies. What does the child consider an emergency? What does the parent consider an emergency? Have a code word that the parent and child can use in the event of any emergency.
- Check in. Call your child while you are away to see how it's going or have a trusted neighbor or friend check in.
- Talk about it. Encourage your child to share his feelings with you about staying home alone. Have this conversation before leaving your child, and when you return, talk with your child about his experiences and feelings while you were away. This is particularly important when your child is first beginning to stay home alone. A quick check-in is always helpful after being away.
- Don't overdo it. Even a mature, responsible child shouldn't be home alone too much. Consider other options, such as programs offered by schools, community centers, youth organizations, or faith-based organizations to help keep your child connected and involved.

The website www.childwelfare.gov also contains a list of state-specific home-alone resources, covering twenty-seven states and the District of Columbia.

Parenting... A Work in Progress

Bullying in Middle Childhood

Bullying is the abuse of physical and psychological power for the purpose of creating intimidation and fear in victims (Zopito, Spear, Bombay, 1999).

Children may be victimized by other children as early as kindergarten. By elementary school, ten percent of students report being harassed by aggressive school mates. Victimization leads to sadness, depression, difficulty controlling anger, and avoidance of school (Ladd et al., 1997).

Bullied children are often shy, have a frail appearance, a history of intrusive and controlling parents, and, among boys, maternal over-protectiveness. "These parenting behaviors prompt anxiety, low self-esteem, and dependency," causing an aura of fear (Berk, 2002, p. 500).

Bullies feed on the fear of others.

> Alex waited with some neighborhood kids for the bus to arrive. The early morning was cold. Alex jumped up and down to get warm. While jumping, the gloves he borrowed from his older sister fell off his hands. Joseph, one of the three students at the bus stop, swept up the gloves and lifted them high into the air.
>
> "Give them back!"
>
> A year older and much larger, Joseph sneered. "No way, peewee, they're mine now. Wait, these are girlie gloves. They have sparkly stuff on them. Here, take 'em back. I don't want no girlie gloves anyway." Joseph packed the gloves with wet snow threw them toward Alex's face. As Alex moved out of the way to avoid

> the blow, he slipped on some ice and fell hard on his bottom. Joseph laughed uncontrollably. Aware crying would make the situation worse, Alex sniffled hard and coughed back his tears.
>
> A scream pierced the air as Alex's mother came rushing forward to yell at Joseph. "You leave my son alone! Your mother won't be happy after I have a talk with her about you." Alex's mother turned to face her son who struggled to get up off the ice. She held out her hand to help him up. "Alex, honey, are you okay?"
>
> "I'm fine. Mom. Look, there's the bus. See you later."
>
> Joseph followed Alex into the bus. "See you later, honey, ha ha."
>
> Joseph chose the seat behind Alex and kicked the bottom of Alex's seat, until Alex found a friend to squeeze next to. It was going to be a tough day.

Since bullying tends to be repetitive, it will not sort itself out and go away without intervention. Over-protectiveness is not the answer, nor is looking at it as a "childhood rite of passage." Strong family support helps.

> Ann moved with her family to a new town just before the school year started. The neighborhood had lots of other children close to her age. No one on her block fenced in their yard, so all the kids ran through each other's properties with enthusiasm. Finally, a kid-friendly place! Not a cranky adult in sight.
>
> Vic lived two houses down the block. He stopped over with his sisters and Max, their golden retriever, the second day Ann moved in. They all seemed nice. The day before, Max trotted over to say hello in his friendliest doggy way. Max was losing his eyesight and thought Ann's dad was the previous owner.
>
> A few days later, Ann ran to her house sobbing.

She stumbled upstairs to her bedroom. Her father saw Ann when she walked past Ann's room. "What's wrong, sweetheart?"

"That guy, Vic, down the street, he won't leave me alone. He keeps bothering me and chasing me. I can't make him stop." Ann hugged her dad and breathed deeply, calming down.

"Well, let's talk about ways to stand up for yourself. Never start a fight, but defend yourself when someone's bullying you." Ann's father put his hands out in front of his body. "Here, punch my hands as hard as you can."

"Dad! I can't do that."

"Sure you can. Practice anyway. No punch harder. Ow! That's enough. You're good to go."

"I don't want to hit anyone!"

"Well, you don't have to. The next time Vic decides to cause you trouble, look him straight in the eye, and run right at him. Odds are he'll run away from you."

"Are you sure?"

"I swear on your mother's cookie-baking ability."

"Oh! You are serious? Mom's cookies are amazing."

"Annie bananie, you're the amazing one."

Ann's parents did not have to wait long for her to try the bully prevention strategy. The following day, Ann's mom and dad were at an upstairs window, looking at the new swing-set they built. Seeing Ann in the backyard, Vic sauntered towards her. Neither parent could hear the conversation. Both wanted to slide the window open and say something but stopped.

Ann looked at Vic and walked towards him fast. Vic turned and ran. Ann ran after Vic until he was in his own yard. Ann walked back home. She felt proud of herself.

Violence to end violence does not work in the long term.

Suggestions to Help Children Deal with Bullies

- Be involved in your children's lives.
- Teach children to stand up for themselves.
- Role model positive ways to deal with conflict.
- Consider classes in self-defense, which include self-discipline.

Sage Advice from Children

The following unattributed advice, from children eight to fourteen, will make you smile.

- "When your dad is mad and asks, 'Do I look stupid?' don't answer him." —Michael, fourteen
- "Never tell your Mom her diet's not working." —Joel, fourteen
- "Stay away from prunes." —Randy, nine
- "When your mom is mad at your dad, don't let her brush your hair." —Emily, ten
- "Don't sneeze in front of your mom when you're eating crackers." —Mitchell, twelve
- "Puppies still have bad breath even after eating a tic-tac." —Andrew, nine
- "Don't pick on your sister when she's holding a baseball bat." —Joel, ten
- "When you get a bad grade, show it to your mom when she's on the telephone." —Alyesha, thirteen
- "Never try to baptize a cat." —Eileen, eight

References For Middle Childhood

Barker, D. J. P. (1994). *Mothers, babies, and disease in later life*. London, UK: British Medical Journal Publishing.

Baumrind, D. (1967). Child care practices anteceding three patterns of preschool behavior. *Genetic Psychology Monographs, 75*, 43-88.

Baumrind, D. (1973). The development of instrumental competence through socialization. In A. Pick (Ed.), *Minnesota Symposium on Child Psychology, 7*. Minneapolis, MN: University of Minnesota Press.

Berk, L. (2002). *Infants, children, and adolescents*. Boston, MA: Allyn & Bacon. (pp. 416-508).

Cairns, G., Angus, K., & Hastings, G. (2009). The extent, nature and effects of food promotion to children: A review of the evidence to December 2008. Geneva, Switzerland: World Health Organization.

Childhelp National Child Abuse Hotline. 800.422.4453. Retrieved from http://www.childhelp.org.

Child Welfare Information Gateway. (2013). *Leaving your child home alone*. Washington, D.C.: U.S. Department of Health and Human Services, Children's Bureau. Retrieved from https://www.childwelfare.gov/pubs/factsheets/homealone.cfm.

CNS Clinic (2007). Cerebral blood flow and oxygen consumption. Retrieved from http://www.humanneurophysiology.com/cbfo2consumption.htm.

Dunn, J. (1996). The Emmanuel Miller Memorial Lecture 1995: Children' relationships: Bridging the divide between cognitive and social development. *Journal of Child Psychology and Psychiatry and Allied Disciplines, 37*, 507-518.

Ezzati, M., Lopez, A. D., Rodgers, A., & Murray, C. J. L. (2004). Comparative quantification of health risks: Global and regional burden of disease attributable to selected major risk factors. Geneva, Switzerland: World Health Organization.

Global status report on noncommunicable diseases 2010 (2011). Geneva, Switzerland: World Health Organization. Available at: http://www.who.int/nmh/publications/ncd_report2010/en/.

Greenwood, B. (2014). The Baumrind theory of parenting styles. *Everyday Life*. Santa Monica, CA: Demand Media. Retrieved from http://everydaylife.globalpost.com/baumrind-theory-parenting-styles-6147.html.

Grinnell, D. (5/07/2012). What's so special about Einstein's brain? *Eureka*. Charles River Laboratories. Retrieved from http://www.criver.com/about-us/eureka/blog/may-2012/.

Hartup, W. W. (1983). Peer relations. In M. Heatherington (Ed.), *Handbook of child psychology, 4*. New York, NY: Wiley

Henry J. Kaiser Foundation (01/2010). *Generation M²: Media in the Lives of 8-18 Year Olds*. Retrieved from http://www.nhlbi.nih.gov/health/educational/wecan/reduce-screen-time/.

Ladd, G. W., Kochenderfer, B. J., & Coleman, C. C. (1997). Classroom peer acceptance, friendship, and victimization: Distinct relational systems that contribute uniquely to children's school adjustment? *Child Development, 68*, 1181-1197.

Legal age restrictions for latchkey kids (2014). Latchkey-Kids.com. Retrieved from http://www.latchkey-kids.com/latchkey-kids-resources.htm

Lobstein, T., Baur, L., & Uauy, R. (2004). Obesity in children and young people: A crisis in public health. *Obesity Reviews, 5*(1), 4-104.

Moskowitz, C. (3/23/2009). Teen brains clear out childhood thoughts. *LiveScience*. Retrieved from http://www.livescience.com/3435-teen-brains-clear-childhood-thoughts.html.

Nannis, E., & Cowen, P. (1987). Emotional understanding: A matter of age, dimension, and point of view. *Journal of Applied Developmental Psychology, 8*(3), 289-304.

U.S. Department of Education, Office of Special Education Programs (2003). Identifying and treating attention deficit hyperactivity disorder: A resource for school and home. Retrieved from http://www.ldonline.org/article/8840/.

NIMH Child Psychiatry Branch (11/12/2007). Brain matures a few years late in ADHD, but follows normal pattern. National Institute of Mental Health. Retrieved from http://www.nimh.nih.gov/news/science-news/2007/brain-matures-a-few-years-late-in-adhd-but-follows-normal-pattern.shtml.

Parker, J. G., & Asher, S. R. (1987). Peer relations and later adjustment: Are low accepted children at risk? *Psychological Bulletin, 102*, 357-389.

Popkin, B. M. (1994). The nutrition transition in low-income countries: An emerging crisis. *Nutrition Review, 52*, 285-298.

Population-based approaches to childhood obesity prevention. World Health Organization, 13, 28. Retrieved from http://www.who.int/dietphysicalactivity/childhood/approaches/en/

Scheeringa, M. S., & Zeanah, C. H. (1995). Symptom expression and trauma variables in children under 48 months of age. *Infant Mental Health Journal, 16*(4), 259-270. Retrieved from http://www.researchgate.net/publication/230127107_Symptom_expression_and_trauma_variables_in_children_under_48_months_of_age.

Scrimshaw, N. S. (05/1997). WFP/UNU Seminar, *The lasting damage of early malnutrition*. Retrieved from http://one.wfp.org/policies/introduction/background/ending/s1.html.

Tsiros, O. T., Buckley, J. D., Grimshaw, P., Brennan, L., Walkley, J., Hills, A. P., Howe, P. R. C., & Coates, A. M. (2009). Health-related quality of life in obese children and adolescents. *International Journal of Obesity, 33*, 387-400.

Toma, John J (07/2014 and 08/2014). Interviews, child development.

Viner R. M., & Cole, T. J. (2005). Television viewing in early childhood predicts adult body mass index. *Journal of Pediatrics, 147*(4), 429–435. Retrieved from http://pediatrics.aappublications.org/content/128/1/201.full.

Williams, J. W. M., Wake, M., Hesketh, K., Maher, E., & Waters, E. (2005). Health-related quality of life of overweight and obese children. *Journal of the American Medical Association, 293*(1), 70-76.

Wolf, J. (n.d.). *Parenting: Single Parents*. About.com. Home Alone Quiz. Retrieved from http://www.about.com.

World Cancer Research Fund/American Institute for Cancer Research (2007). Food, nutrition, physical activity, and the prevention of cancer: A global perspective. Washington, D.C.: AICR.

Zopito, M., Spear, S., & Bombay, K. (1999). Peer victimization in middle childhood: Characteristics, causes, and consequences of school bullying. *Brock Education Journal, 9*(1), 33. Retrieved from http://brock.scholarsportal.info/journals/brocked/home/article/view/329/205.

Middle Childhood Further Reading

Armstrong, T. (2009). *Multiple intelligences in the classroom*. Alexandria, VA: Association for Supervision and Curriculum Development.

Benson, E. (2003). Intelligence across cultures. *American Psychological Association, 34*(2). Retrieved from http://www.apa.org/monitor/feb03/intelligence.aspx.

Cherry, K. (n.d.). Social and emotional milestones: Important milestones in social and emotional development. *Education: Psychology*. About.com. Retrieved from http://psychology.about.com/od/early-child-development/a/social-and-emotional-milestones.htm.

Dangx111 (11/05/2011). *The four parenting styles*. Retrieved from http://blog.lib.umn.edu/meyer769/myblog/2011/11/the-four-types-of-parenting-styles.html.

Downsizing a super-sized problem: Curbing childhood obesity. *American Academy of Pediatrics: Healthy Children*. (7/09/2014). Retrieved from http://www.healthychildren.org/English/healthy-living/nutrition/Pages/Healthy-Active-Living-for-Families.aspx.

Hatter, K. (2014). Aggressive behavior in children under 5 years of age. *Everyday Life Global Post*. Retrieved from http://everydaylife.

globalpost.com/aggressive-behavior-children-under-5-years-age-4697.html.

Kutner, L. (2007). Aggressive children. *Psych Central*. Retrieved from http://psychcentral.com/lib/aggressive-children/0001221.

Mannheim, J. K. (updated 11/09/2012). *School-age children development: Physical development*. Retrieved from http://www.nlm.nih.gov/medlineplus/ency/article/002017.htm.

Morin, A. (n.d.). The difference between consequences and punishments for kids. Learn how to teach your child to learn from mistakes. *Parenting: Discipline*. About.com. Retrieved from http://discipline.about.com/od/disciplinebasics/a/The-Difference-Between-Consequences-And-Punishments-For-Kids.htm.

Multiple intelligence theory. (n.d.). *SPARKed*. Retrieved from http://www.kqed.org/assets/pdf/arts/programs/spark/multipleintelligences.pdf?trackurl=true

Positive parenting tips for healthy child development, middle childhood (6-8 years of age). National Center on Birth Defects and Developmental Disabilities Division of Human Development and Disability (last reviewed 3/11/2014). Retrieved from http://www.cdc.gov/ncbddd/childdevelopment/positiveparenting/pdfs/middlechildhood6-8.pdf

Physical activity tools and resources (11/08/2013). National Heart, Lung, and Blood Institute. Retrieved from http://www.nhlbi.nih.gov/health/educational/wecan/tools-resources/physical-activity.htm.

Toma, John J. Ph.D. Neuropsychology. Biltmore Evaluation and Treatment Services. Phoenix.

Van Jaarsveld, A. W. (04/2007). *Divorce and children in middle childhood: Parents' contribution to minimize the impact* (Magister Socialis Deligentiae dissertation). University of Pretoria, South Africa.

Wolf, J. (2014). At what age can I leave my children home alone? Guidelines for single parent families. *Parenting: Single Parents*. About.com. Retrieved from http://singleparents.about.com/od/havingfun/f/homealone.htm.

Wolf, J. (2014). Is your child ready to stay home alone? Put your mind at ease with this interactive quiz. *Parenting: Single Parents*. Retrieved from http://singleparents.about.com/library/quiz/bl_home_alone_quiz.htm.

Parenting... A Work in Progress

Section 4

ADOLESCENCE—
AGES TWELVE THROUGH YOUNG ADULT

During adolescence, the teen's body clock changes by about two hours. A child who normally woke at 7 a.m. would have a time shift to wake up at 9 a.m. It's no wonder so many teens are sleepy in high school.

The development of the adolescent's prefrontal cortex allows her to think abstractly. She no longer takes what parents say as fact. She compares and contrasts what behaviors and rules other parents allow to what her own parents feel is appropriate. Adolescents feel smarter than their parents. Teens question everything—not necessarily a bad thing. Questioning shows teens are thinking for themselves.

Risk taking, often with input from friends, seems to be part of the path of adolescent development. Teens believe nothing bad will ever happen to them. Bad things happen to other people.

Emotional distance and conflict between children and parents increase during adolescence (Steinberg, 1989). Social interaction with peers increases. This may help teens develop more social skills away from home, allowing them opportunity to practice independent behavior (Spear, 2000). Teenagers strive to develop their own identities separate

Parenting... A Work in Progress

from family. They want to know why they need to follow family rules that do not make sense to them.

- Why do I have to go to church?
- Why do I have to be in this religion?
- Why can't I stay out late?
- Why do I have to tell you everywhere I go and who I'm with?
- Why do I have to agree with your political views?

Despite the emotional pullback from family, adolescents have a strong need for acceptance. They are easily pressured by peers and what they see in all types of media. Open communication between parents and adolescents is the first line of defense. Listen to your teens, and they will listen to you.

Brain Development and Thinking in Adolescence

"Who are you and what have you done to my child?"

It is the parents' job to guide their children, but parenting has never been simple. Crypts found in the Wailing Wall, or West Wall, in Jerusalem from the 11th century contain prayers with parents asking for help with their teenagers who are "dressing funny" and "fornicating" (Toma, 2014).

Perhaps your child has been easy going. Overnight you find yourself faced with an argumentative creature who looks exactly like your child but couldn't possibly be the same person. What happened? Some vague remembrance from your own coming of age creeps back and whispers to you, "Hormones?" No, the brain is restructuring. The child's prefrontal cortex is completing development and preparing to integrate experience. Due to the intense changes in the brain, the child's behaviors are actually physically prompted.

The prefrontal cortex allows for abstract thinking. Now the child compares and contrasts information. Instead of taking what parents say as truth, they fact-check with others. It happens to everyone.

> The sixth grade class rode the bus back from a field trip. On the way down Main Street, Alex pointed out of a window. "Hey look, Mario, it's Hooters! They have the best hot-wings ever."
>
> Mario's eyes widened. "What? My mom told me you have to be eighteen years old to go to Hooters."
>
> "No, man. You can go. We go there all the time."

Mario, whose mother feels offended by the restaurant's uniforms, has fact-checked with his friend whose parents have no problem taking the family to Hooters. Mario will have a difficult time believing his mother in the future and will fact-check more often. Honesty is a better approach. Mario is old enough to understand other people's feelings.

"But I can't do math!"

> Amy desperately wanted to learn how to play piano. There was not enough room in the house or budget for a full-sized piano, so her parents picked up a full-sized electronic keyboard on a stand. Before taking music lessons, Amy found math classes difficult. One side effect of music lessons was a change in the way she approached her math homework. For some reason it was not as difficult. The math made more sense and was less frustrating.

In his book, *The Math Gene*, Keith Devlin points out that both musicians and mathematicians use abstract notation to describe on paper the patterns they "see" in their mind. A trained musician reading musical symbols moves straight to "hearing" in his mind the sounds that the symbols represent. A trained mathematician reading mathematical symbols moves directly to thinking about the patterns that the symbols represent.

The potential for mathematical and musical neural pathways to complement each other exists if your child keeps practicing that guitar (Gupta, 3/11/ 2009).

"Whether your child practices and composes music daily, or just enjoys dancing around the house to music, providing the right music for the right purpose can help your child learn in general but potentially excel at mathematics" (Gupta). Baroque music helps children to focus and concentrate. Mozart is energetic and keeps children alert. Children memorize more easily when putting facts to music or rhyme.

The students in Mrs. Albright's sixth grade math class sat down and began the work that was printed on the board. Geometry was the new topic. The students struggled to memorize the formulas for area and perimeter of basic shapes. Physical models would have helped, but state exams were coming fast, and students weren't allowed to use the models during the test.

Pete raised his hand. "Mrs. Albright, I am having a hard time remembering all the formulas. They're getting jumbled up in my mind."

Other students voiced the same concern.

Mrs. Albright smiled. "I've been thinking about this and have an idea. Does any of you have a method to use for remembering your phone number?"

Several students' hands shot up.

"Yes, Jenny?"

"My little sister uses "Twinkle, Twinkle, Little Star" to remember the phone number. My mom has a good one. She uses Katy Perry's "Roar" to remember a new phone number. Sometimes I do, too."

"Class, look up here please. Here's what we're going to do. I'll write the formulas for area and perimeter of the circle, square, triangle, and rhombus on the board. You're going to work in groups of three and write songs with dance moves that go with two of the shapes on the board. You can choose your own group, as long as we keep the noise level down."

"Mrs. Albright, you are all right!" two students chimed.

"See, you are already thinking in terms of rhyming lyrics. Get started everyone."

It doesn't matter what instrument or type of music your child learns. The process of learning is what helps, and not just in math. According to psychologist Dr. Agnes Chan, "Learning music stimulates the left temporal lobe . . . which is the area of the brain responsible for verbal memory" (Ho et al., 2003). Children who receive musical training have better recall of words than those who receive none.

"Stop, you are making me think too hard. My head hurts!"

Thinking uses a lot of energy. Using the brain and the rest of the body causes changes within both. Learn a new group of physical exercises and your body changes to accommodate. Muscles may hurt for a time, while your body changes. With practice, muscles grow stronger, and the physical exercises become less strenuous.

The same is true for learning an academic skill. The brain uses tremendous energy when learning a new task. Your head may ache. With practice, just as with physical exercise, the academic skill becomes easier. The brain requires less energy to do the task.

All-nighters just before a test are not recommended, as the brain needs more time to sift through the information being introduced to it. Studying short chunks of information over several days is a more successful strategy than studying the day before a test. Anxiety causes difficulties retrieving information from memory. A calm mind works better.

The students in my psychology class entered the room and prepared to take their mid-term exam. As part of the course, I taught relaxation techniques. One method was especially useful in the midst of many people. It involved closing the eyes, taking slow, deep breaths, and picturing a "happy place." Where that place happened to be was of no consequence.

> Frieda, one of my students, walked in just before the bell rang, looking frantic.
>
> I spoke to the class. "All books closed and under your seats, please. The only items to be on your desks are pencil or pen. When you receive your exam papers, please keep them face down. We will all start at the same time. When you begin, please check that you have all four pages of the test. If not, raise your hand

> and I will give you another exam."
>
> The students began working. Frieda slumped in her chair, staring at her test paper with a flat expression. She looked up to see where I was and raised her hand. I motioned for her to follow me to the doorway where we spoke quietly. "Frieda, you look lost. Is everything okay?"
>
> "Ms. B, I studied all the material for the test and know it, but my mind has gone totally blank. I can't remember anything!"
>
> "Okay, Frieda. Let's look at the first question. Tell me about Lev Vygotsky's zone of proximal development."
>
> Frieda talked to me about Lev Vygotsky and realized all she needed to do was relax. Her memory returned.
>
> "Thanks, Ms. B, I'm okay now."

Stepping away from a problem and relaxing allows some higher functions of the brain to work without the stress of worrying about the problem. Worrying freezes our ability to move forward towards a solution.

My students have mentioned that I've made their heads hurt from thinking too much. That's a good thing. They're stretching brain capacity and becoming more intelligent! The human brain and body are always in a state of change. People are capable of growth at all ages. Your child's intelligence level is going to change. It might go up or down. Keep in mind that standardized tests are just that: a standard for comparison. The test scores only show what your child accomplished the day of testing—not necessarily what the child knows. The scores change according to hours slept, hunger, whatever happened on the way to school, what happened at home before they left for school, who said what to whom. All factor into testing, because these things matter on a daily basis. No one lives in a vacuum. Human beings are the product of their environment and genes.

The current culture decides what is considered intelligent or valuable to society. There will always be bias and expectations. Parents and teachers need to remember that both heredity and environment contribute to children's wellbeing and success in life.

William Woolston did an interesting study in October 2008 called "Do Great Expectations" Matter? The Relationship between Teacher Expectations and Student Academic Success" for The Institute for Research on Education Policy & Practice Stanford University. Woolston showed that the teacher's perceived view of his or her students' attendance was an important indicator of student success.

Teachers who overestimated a student's absence were pessimistic about that student's likelihood to enroll in college. This had nothing to do with the student's actual attendance. It was the teacher's perception. If the teacher believed the student would probably attend college, the student's test scores increased. Possible influences may have been setting higher standards, giving more individualized time, and positively reinforcing hard work.

Unexpected was the finding that, while teacher expectations are important for all subjects and for all students, they appear to matter most for girls and in math.

Parents and teachers should work as partners and communicate often. If children know they are appreciated for their efforts, they will be more likely to succeed.

"Gotta dance, gotta sing, I have a funny story for you!"

For many years I worked as a Resource Specialist Program (RSP) teacher. Some of my most rewarding teaching moments happened while working in the RSP classroom. This position required patience, flexibility, and a real love for working with people who think and learn in unusual ways. One of my students insisted that the schools had it all wrong. School should be for two days, and the remaining five should be a long weekend.

My students taught me to appreciate unusual methods to arrive at answers. Many of the RSP students have been full-body, tactile learners. They taught me the importance of knowing them well as individuals, not just people to spoon feed information. I found keeping an open mind and paying close attention to be imperative when working with differently abled students.

> Robert was funny. He was also a gifted artist. He had some difficulty reading. We made a deal and announced it to the room. If Robert came up with a really good joke—only one per day—everyone in the Resource room would stop what they were doing and listen to his joke. We would all laugh and then get back to work. This broke up the time a bit but was well worth the interruptions. Robert felt good about himself, started enjoying school more (although he still felt the weekend should be longer), and relaxed enough to be able to work on his reading skills. The joke break served as a creative outlet that took the place of other attention-getting behavior.
>
> Since he had the approval of the teacher, he gained the approval of the other students. Later in the year, when one of the students was having trouble drawing, she asked Robert for help. He jumped right in, gave her some suggestions, and helped with part of the drawing. Robert's parents knew what I was doing in the classroom. Communication and working as a team to help the children was of utmost importance. We all worked together to help Robert help himself.

"Wait, didn't I ask you to clean the bathroom sink and throw your dirty clothes into the hamper?"

Life is busy. There are only so many hours in a day, and there is never enough time. It is frustrating to ask your teen to do a few chores then find him waiting for further instructions, chores half done. Why is this so difficult? What were they thinking? Were they thinking at all?

> "Samuel, I need you to wash the windows in the living room."

> Samuel's mother left the house to do some grocery shopping. An hour later she returned to find the windows half done—literally. Samuel had only washed the lower half of each window. "Sam! Seriously? What on this green earth made you think I only wanted the bottom half of the windows cleaned?"
>
> "I don't know." Samuel panicked. He walked backwards, bumping into the stepstool his mother left so he could reach the top half of the windows. "Oh. I guess I forgot about the stepstool. I couldn't reach the top half. Sorry."

The organized thinking required for multi-tasking develops roughly from thirteen to seventeen. Better to keep tasks limited to avoid frustrations on everybody's part.

This means you may have a child who has mastered driver's education but may not be capable of juggling all the thoughts needed to successfully maneuver the complexities of the roadways. Practice will make a huge difference, especially with someone calm sitting alongside your child. If parents feel uncomfortable teaching children to drive, better to have someone else help.

The Highway or No Way

> Alice's father did not want her to drive, but he still allowed her to sign up for driver's education. The high school Alice attended did not offer driver's education, so she took it during the summer at another school. Taking a summer class was not her idea of fun, but she wanted to learn how to drive.
>
> Alice passed the driving and classroom portions of the class. She got her driver's permit! Now all she had to do was get her father to help practice driving so she would be able to pass the driver's exam and get her license! Alice thought, "Too bad Mom's so busy with work. She's not as cranky."

Alice was fortunate to get her father to take her driving five times that year. It was the day before her 16th birthday. Alice begged her father, "Please let me practice. I have to take the road test by tomorrow!" Alice suspected her mother made him go out for a last practice before the test.

Their family lived near the entrance to a busy highway. Her father asked her to turn right on the main road. Alice felt nervous. Her father then directed her towards the most difficult highway entrance. It was a left-sided entry onto very fast traffic.

"I don't want to drive on the highway Dad!"

Alice was told, in no uncertain terms, she would drive on the highway right then or forget about her license.

It was a poor bluff.

Alice turned right and proceeded down the ramp and into the busy traffic, directly into the left fast lane.

"Press the gas pedal! Oh my God!" Her father clung onto the dashboard. "Get over to the right lane. No, not yet. Look where you're going!"

She managed, by some miracle, to maneuver to the far right lane and get off the highway at the next exit. Alice was angry—never a good state of mind for driving.

"Okay, now you have a lead-foot," her father said. "Where was it on the highway?"

Alice slowed down and continued to drive. By this time her father had stopped screaming and asked her if she had any idea where she was.

"No."

Her father gave her directions, one at a time, until they arrived at the house. To this day she has no idea how the conversation went between her parents, but the following day, Alice's father drove her to the testing facility where she passed her test and received her license.

> Alice listened and maneuvered the car as requested but did not remember where she had driven. Alice's fury interfered with her brain's ability to recall where she drove that evening. Anger clouds decisions, making it difficult to see anything clearly. It was impossible for Alice to multi-task while her mind raged.

Organized thinking, necessary for multi-tasking, is an advanced skill that develops during adolescence and continues into adulthood. Driving a vehicle, particularly in an urban or busy suburban area, requires the ability to focus and keep track of several activities at once. Stringent rules about who should be in a car with a new driver and how many people should be allowed make perfect sense.

Tempting as it may be to ask a child to multi-task or use multiple steps before she is developmentally able is futile and frustrating to parent and child. No amount of yelling and restating the multiple step requests will help. A parent might consider occasionally testing the waters to see if the child is ready to pay attention and remember more than two steps. Although the child may not be ready due to immaturity of the area of the brain responsible for organized thinking, a patient parent may help the child develop this important life skill.

If the steps are directly related to each other and familiar to the child, multi-step directions will be easier to "chunk" or group together. A request to turn off the computer and the lights in the bedroom before bed will be easier to remember than asking him to replace the water in the humidifier and brush his teeth before bed. The computer and lights are both electronic and happen to be in the same room. Replacing water in the humidifier takes more than one step in itself, and the humidifier is probably not in the same room as the toothbrush. Related tasks are simple to group together, so they are easier to remember.

When all else fails, maintaining a sense of humor and remembering to breathe calmly will help keep parents sane during the adolescent years.

To Sleep, Perhaps, To Dream

"Please, just five more minutes."

How many times have you heard, "Just five more minutes, then I'll get up, I promise."

Time passes. Still no movement from the bedroom. Ken wakes up his drowsy, cranky, sleep-deprived teen. The rush for the day is on! "Get dressed and ready for school," he says as he's walking toward the kitchen. "Albi, No! There's no way you're leaving the house dressed like that. Wait, have some breakfast!"

Albert is out and gone. Ken hopes a call won't come from the school office stating his son has fallen asleep in class. Again.

There is debate about the length of time an adolescent requires for a good night's sleep. Between seven and a half and nine and a half hours are suggested. As everyone's body needs are different, it makes perfect sense that sleep requirements will change to fit the individual. No one person is average. If you wake up tired, there's either too much stress in life or you aren't getting enough sleep.

Internal Clock Shift

A biological shift in the internal clock of an adolescent happens after puberty. The adolescent body clock adjusts by approximately two hours (Adapted from: Mindell J. A. & Owens J. A., 2003). If your teenager's waking hours were seven A.M. to ten P.M., the waking schedule changes to nine A.M. until midnight.

Teens may be up late texting, working, playing online, or studying. Sadly, high schools frequently start the school day early. Many teens are barely able to function when they arrive. Sleepy students are moody, have poor reaction time, poor judgment, and are inattentive. The following suggestions may help.

- Keep the bedroom dark. It's hard to sleep when the sun is visible or a streetlight is shining through a window.
- Go to bed and wake up at the same time every day.
- Meditate or nap for a short time after getting home from school.
- Avoid stimulating activities, food, or drink prior to bedtime.

It is generally not good to consume caffeine before bed, as it will keep many people awake. On the other hand, some adults who were highly active as children self-medicate with coffee throughout the day. It keeps them relaxed and better able to focus. Stimulants like caffeine, that keep non-hyperactive people awake if consumed late, have the opposite effect on hyperactive people. To a hyperactive individual, stimulants are calming. This would be a topic to discuss with your child's health care provider.

Snoring and Sleep Apnea

Snoring in sleep is a great concern. Snoring happens for a number of reasons, one being overweight. Sometimes losing some weight will cause snoring to lessen or stop altogether.

Sleep apnea, the stoppage of breath during sleep, can accompany snoring. Apnea sounds like a sharp intake of breath followed by partial waking. The many mini-disturbances sleep apnea causes make people feel tired, even though they may have had an average night's sleep. Sleep apnea is dangerous and should be brought to the attention of a physician immediately.

> Maria, a student, frequently looked tired. The teacher spoke with Maria's mother, who said her daughter ate little and slept poorly. The teacher and her assistant said in unison, "Does Maria have sleep apnea? You should talk to her pediatrician."

Teachers cannot diagnose sleep apnea or other problems. They can make suggestions. The doctor said Maria did have sleep apnea and recommended both her tonsils and adenoids be removed. After the surgery, the apnea stopped. She had better rest during sleep, and her appetite picked up.

"Earth calling . . . Hey, where did you go anyway?"

Daydreams

Daydreams play an important role in our lives. Daytime dreams may:
- Help to relieve stress.
- Help us escape the daily routine without leaving the building
- Assist in creativity.

Most people daydream, especially at times when attention can be freed from the tasks at hand. A University of British Columbia study found that when we daydream, brain areas linked to complex problem solving, which were once thought to be dormant during daydreaming, are more active in the daydream state than when we focus on a routine task (Christoff et al., 2009). The brain is highly active during daydreams.

Why do we dream?

In sleep we grow, heal, and work out problems that occurred during our waking hours. We visit with loved ones, live through anxieties, and solve problems. Brain activity is greater during sleep than when awake. We dream, even though we do not always remember we have dreamed. Dreaming is important for our wellbeing. Dreams may help us weave past experiences with the present to help understand the future.

We sort out problems while we sleep. A teaching assistant, seeing her student's frustration while learning calculus, explained what she did when she encountered a puzzling problem. "First I cry. Then I fall asleep. By the time I wake up, the problem is solved!" The puzzle sorted itself out while she slept.

Rest is necessary for the body and brain. Without enough sleep, the ability to think clearly is compromised. Daytime problems may be solved in sleep. Dreaming helps the mind make sense of daily experiences. Daydreams increase creativity levels for everyone.

Peer Pressure in Adolescence

"But it seemed like a good idea at the time!"

When is an adolescent going to get into trouble most often? While hanging out with friends, of course! Teens do things with their friends that they would never consider on their own. Much like herd mentality, one drifts off the range and the others follow. Moo.

> Paula, Cindy, and Lani decided to start a club. Paula thought there should be some sort of ritual involved in joining the club. She brought out a dead bird her younger brother found underneath the back porch of her house. "Here, sniff this. No, sniff really hard." This was the initiation.
>
> Shortly after all of them had officially joined the club by sniffing the bird, they began sneezing.
>
> Cindy looked at Paula and Lani in horror and said, "Hurry, get some tissue! There's black stuff coming out of your nose!"
>
> Paula dropped the dead bird on the ground and ran into her house. She came back with a roll of toilet paper. "Here! This is all I could find." The girls blew their noses. Black particles came out. They feared none of them would ever be normal again.
>
> Lani was really scared. She passed the roll of toilet paper to Cindy who had the same trouble. Each girl started to cry.
>
> "I'll be right back. I'll get more toilet paper from

> home," Lani called, as she ran down the block, terrified someone would notice what she had done. She tried to control her emotions and hide her feelings. She crept into the house without being seen, grabbed what she needed, and ran back to Paula's backyard. After what seemed hours, the girls stopped sneezing and clearing their noses. All three were too frightened to tell their parents. None of them knew what caused the black bird's death. Paula, Cindy, and Lani were fortunate not to have become ill.
>
> The black particles were dirt and dust that had accumulated on the dead bird. The real danger lay in the cause of the bird's death. If it had been bacterial in nature, the girls may have been in trouble.

Planning, Impulse Control, and Rational Thinking

The last part of the brain to mature is involved in planning, impulse control, and rational thinking (Selemon, 3/05/2013). Not having reached maturity, the adolescent girls agreed to inhale a dead bird's body without considering any consequences. Their only rational idea was the thought to get tissue. It would be several years before the prefrontal cortex, the part of the brain that keeps risk-taking behavior in control, would be fully developed.

Adolescents are more influenced by their peers than their parents. Risk taking, often with input from friends, seems to be part of the predetermined path of neural development. It is no wonder that adolescents are frequently at odds with the adults in their lives.

Since risky behavior appears to be hard-wired in the development of adolescents, it makes sense to look for positive ways to channel the need to take risks. Social reward is important—more important than any possible negative, if negatives are even considered (Helfinstein & Poldrack, 2012).

Positive Peer Pressure

Many adolescents feel insecure. Adolescence is a time of high drama. No one wants to be embarrassed in front of their friends, particularly at this age.

Peer pressure is not always a bad thing. A friend may decide to join a group of people that get together to clean up a neighborhood park so it would be a friendlier place for the younger children to play. The positive peer influence to do something prosocial may cause the teen to join, doing good work for the community. Social recognition is important to adolescents.

Teenagers need immediate rewards and are not concerned with risks. They are in a phase of life where they believe they will live forever. *"Nothing will happen to me!"* They are impulsive and have difficulty resisting pressure from peers. Parents still have influence on adolescents, especially if they paid attention to them when they were younger.

Teens will listen to you if you listen to them. Communication runs two ways. Teens will thank their parents later, often when they have children of their own.

Media Influence

"But I'm supposed to look like them."

Children spend more time using media than any other waking activity. Whatever they are exposed to will affect their thoughts about the world around them, as well as their views of themselves. Anyone who does the research is aware that adolescents are body conscious and highly susceptible to suggestion. Note the plethora of commercials and other advertisements about hair, skin, clothes, body size, and odor.

Adolescents' need to be accepted is strong. While reading magazines at local drug stores and grocery stores, patrons may find many articles about the next great diet. "Eat this and lose ten pounds in one week, no exercise needed! You too can have flat abs this summer!" Extreme diets are stressful on the body and often unsuccessful. Gradual change is healthier and longer lasting. Families do better to stress the importance of fitness and diet for a healthy life.

> Addie, a happy twelve year old, was not overweight, but she had not had a growth spurt in a while. Her mom, Janet, felt concerned about Addie's size for her height. When Janet was the same age as her daughter, Janet's father mentioned that she ought to eat less.
>
> "Just eat until you think you need a little more food; then stop. Oh, and remember to chew all your food twenty eight times before you swallow. Your hips are as big as a grown-up adult. Better watch yourself, girl."
>
> Watch herself was exactly what she did. Too well. Janet wondered what she could say without making

> Addie feel bad about herself. The last thing Janet wanted was to damage her daughter's sense of self and her body image, knowing how self-conscious one can become when criticized, especially when fault has been found by a parent. Janet kept her thoughts to herself. One afternoon Addie brought home a flier from school that described several after-school activities.
>
> "This looks like fun Addie. How about soccer?"
>
> When she was older, Addie looked at pictures of herself at age twelve. Had her mom pointed out her concern with weight, Addie would have remembered that time with little warmth. Her mother's choice to gently suggest physical activity helped Addie retain her good sense of self.

Body Image

Body image is an especially important matter to preteens and teenagers. Adolescents are sensitive to the pressures of society. Messages sent via electronic and print media bombard them with photos of unrealistic body types. Retouched photographs are everywhere. These unrealistic images of people are what our society, influenced by advertising, has deemed to be the ideal body type. It is a false representation of reality. There are no real-life Barbie and Ken dolls walking about.

Eating Disorder - Bulimia

> Sarah Wilson and her son, CJ, drove to the dentist's office.
>
> "CJ, the dentist said last time that your teeth were showing some signs of wear. Are you grinding your teeth in your sleep?"
>
> "Mom, you worry too much. I'm fine. It's no big deal."
>
> "CJ, if something is bothering you, I hope you know you can always talk to me."

> "Sure, Mom. Let's get this over with. I've got soccer practice this afternoon."
>
> Sarah and CJ sat in the waiting room for a few minutes. Dr. Simmons walked towards mother and son. "Mrs. Wilson, CJ, good to see you! Come on back, and we'll see how things are progressing."
>
> After the exam, Dr. Simmons said, "Mrs. Wilson, I am concerned about your son's teeth. I am seeing a greater-than-expected loss of enamel. CJ, have you been vomiting frequently?" CJ thought about it. "No. Well, yeah . . . but the other guys on the team do it too. It's no big deal."
>
> CJ had been bingeing and purging more than a year, trying to keep his weight down. He was working on a six-pack muscle group and wanted to look buff. All he succeeded in doing was to make himself look puffier. Before the alert from the family dentist, Sarah had no idea. CJ had been careful about stashing the empty ice cream containers he consumed in one sitting directly into the trash bin outside.

Health Consequences

Bulimia—binge eating and purging—is an eating disorder, a serious emotional and physical problem that is life threatening. Anyone may become a victim of this disorder. The longer an individual waits to get help, the more costly in terms of health and finance.

John Ford, DDS, in private practice in the Chicago area, suggests seeking help from a university dental school. "The university dental schools are affiliated with the medical schools and have all the disciplines in the same place. A person with an eating disorder is going to need psychological, medical, and dental assistance. At this type of campus, all professionals are able to discuss the patient. This way the patient receives the best, most comprehensive care. A post-graduate with a specialist will work on the case.

"When someone purges, hydrochloric acid bathes the back of the teeth—the tops and somewhat on the bottom. Usually, the front six to eight teeth are affected. The patient's bite changes, the esophagus may be damaged, and crowns will be needed on all teeth after the patient receives psychiatric help. The total mouth rebuild takes a year or more of treatment. It is a huge expense."

Children with eating disorders are frequently intelligent and want to please. They work diligently in school and are often hard on themselves. There is a strong need to control, sometimes eased by where, when, and what is eaten. Eating disorders begin as a method to control at least one aspect of life. In the end, without help, the disorder is in control.

Attractiveness Through History

Women were designed to ensure the survival of their children, which early in human history involved remaining healthy through times of famine. Full-figured women were considered attractive, as they were likely to survive during scarcity of food. Women have a greater percentage of fat cells and fewer fat releasing enzymes than men, making weight loss difficult and weight gain easier—for the survival of our species (Lockwood et al., 2000).

The definitive, ideal body type changes with the times. From the 16th century through the early 1900s, corsets were in demand, when the hourglass figure was the ideal look for women. Different styles of corsets, long and short, redefined female body shape. During the 1960s and early '70s, women starved their way through a skeletal phase. The 21st century body ideal suggests a muscular, toned appearance for both men and women.

How Parents Can Help

Parents can show their children, who are trying so hard to fit in, that they look beautiful as they are.

- Stress a healthy lifestyle.
- Exercise as a family.
- Have more family meals and talk to each other.

Even if there is the occasional eye-roll, what parents say and how they respond is meaningful to the children. It may take them until they turn thirty to thank you, so have patience. Although peer pressure is strong, parents can and do make a positive difference. Be vigilant! Keep healthy foods in the house, and make sure you eat them too. You are being watched. Children don't miss a thing.

> Angela's three-year-old son, Ben, the love of her life, adored his mommy and followed her everywhere. One evening after dinner, Angela, horrified, watched as Ben stuck his finger down his throat after eating. After all, that's what Mommy did. Angela had not realized her need to purge would be copied by her baby boy. She tried so hard to be secretive. The incident prompted Angela to get help. Ben never saw his mommy put her fingers down her throat again.

Parent's habits may become their children's choice.

Watch television with your children. Dissect programs and advertisements together. Show them you value their opinions. Take time for your children now. There will come a time when they will need someone to listen to them. If parents show that they care about their children by paying attention now, their children will listen to them later.

Social Media in Adolescence

Cyber Life Calling

Social media offers information and allows readers to participate in the content. With social media, we have the ability to make contacts and share ideas and pictures with people all over the world. Corporations, advertisers, educational institutions, and governments use social media. Gauging consumer opinion helps organizations know how best to grow and profit.

Facebook, YouTube, LinkedIn, Pinterest, and Twitter consume our attention.

- The weather is horrific by my mom's house, and I can't reach her by phone. Does anyone know what's going on in that area of the country?
- Does anyone have any idea how to make gluten-free pizza that actually tastes good?
- Has anyone seen my dog? Hercules, my teacup Chihuahua, has been missing since the last tornado.

The ability to reach out anywhere, at any time and place, if coverage is available, and say whatever is on your mind is enticing.

Social media has many positives. It provides opportunities to learn about other people's interests in food, music, sports, and local activities. Teens may have difficulties with social interaction or feel socially awkward but often feel more comfortable using social media than speaking face to face. Social media helps teach interpersonal skills, such as empathy. Many teens use social networks to gather information and advice.

According to a report by Pauline Dakin of CBC News, using digital communication may cause fewer personal connections with others. Intimacy is related to self-disclosure. Using social media adolescents are self-disclosing to hundreds.

About 75 percent of adolescents own cell phones, and almost all of them text. Teens text thousands of times per month. Intimate in-person friendships may be going the way of "likes" to posts and Facebook statuses. Emotional support is being given by large numbers of network online friends who have never meet in real life (Salimkhan et al., 2010).

The American Academy for Pediatrics policy statement offers recommendations for parents regarding screen use, including:

- Parents can model effective "media diets" to help their children learn to be selective and healthy in what they consume. Take an active role in children's media education by co-viewing programs with them and discussing values.
- Make a media use plan, including mealtime and bedtime curfews for media devices. Screens should be kept out of kids' bedrooms.
- Limit entertainment screen time to less than one or two hours per day; in children under two, eliminate screen media exposure, when possible.

See more at: http://www.aap.org/en-us/about-the-aap/aap-press-room/Pages/Managing-Media-We-Need-a-Plan.aspx - sthash.L2zpPhOF.dpuf

In addition to social media engaging too much time and causing loss of sleep, real dangers like cyber stalking and cyber bullying also exist.

Cyber Bullying in Adolescence

Adolescents don't have the emotional filters most adults possess. Teens and preteens have a tendency towards impulsivity. Tweets can be taken the wrong way and cause altercations later. Online forums may engender unpleasant remarks. Some may be cruel.

> David was oblivious to a website created all about him. For months there had been a website that made fun of David and his family. The site said things like he was a pedophile, he was gay and dirty and invited others to actively bash this boy. Along with the website, people sent David hateful emails telling him how much they didn't like him.
>
> When some girls stole Amanda's belongings, she reported it. Later that night, she received instant messages calling her harsh names and saying she was a tattletale. Trying to defend herself, she replied that they had stolen her stuff. That just made it worse. She received more internet messages. All mean. The girls never said another word to her in person.
>
> An autistic thirteen-year-old became the prime target of cyber bullying. He had a crush. The girl stood up for him for a while but soon became the main bully. She pretended to like him and then made fun of him and said she would never like a guy like him. As his pain became worse, an internet pen pal encouraged him to end his life. Ryan became despondent. He hung himself, all because of cyber-bullies (NOBullying.com, 2014).

Parenting... A Work in Progress

Many cases of cyber bullying begin from home over the computer or smartphone and continue the following day in school.

> Frank and Olivia, both eighth grade students in the same high school, dated for a few months. Frank decided he no longer wanted to see Olivia and broke up with her. Olivia, despondent, called her friend, Kaye. "Frank dumped me. I can't believe it! What an idiot. Do you think he's seeing someone else?"
>
> Kaye was thankful Olivia called instead of coming over. She couldn't face Olivia. Kaye had started seeing Frank last Saturday. "Uh . . . no. I don't think he's seeing anyone. You know Frank. He's such a flake."
>
> "I guess so. Boys . . . they just don't get it."
>
> Several weeks went past. Olivia walked down the hallway. Turning a corner she saw Frank with his arm around Kaye's shoulder. Kaye was too close to Frank. Olivia blushed. "Hey, that's my boyfriend!"
>
> "He is not!"
>
> Frank, sensing major drama, stepped away from Kaye. "I'm outta here. I've got class." He walked away. The assistant principal walked down the hallway before either girl could continue the conversation.
>
> "Girls, the bell rings in two minutes. Better get to class."
>
> Both girls were agitated but could do nothing about it. At home, Kaye signed in to her Facebook account and posted a nasty story about Olivia and what she did with Frank—all untrue. The following day at school, Olivia, who had not checked her Facebook account, wondered why many of the students smiled and sniggered at her.
>
> Kaye's friend, Linda, bumped into Olivia's shoulder. "Hey, be careful, Linda. That hurt!"
>
> "Not as much as you'll hurt when you see Facebook. I know what you did." Linda walked past Olivia.

> "What? Hey, get back here, you b**ch."
> The assistant principal got to the girls as they were pulling each other's hair. "Counselor's office, now!"

A Successful School Approach

A school in Nevada has a tiered discipline policy for cyber bullying. In the worst case, students who cyber bully may find themselves expelled from school.

First, the administrators of the school call the students involved for mediation. This is viewed as punishment by the students, as the cyber attacker and attacked do not want real-life, upfront confrontation. Parents are contacted immediately after mediation. This is a team effort, so parents must always be kept in the loop.

The next step is a four-hour Saturday detention at the school site. The student pays a fee to help defray the cost of adult supervision. During detention, students work around the campus, scraping gum off desks, pulling weeds, and generally helping to make their school a more beautiful campus. Depending upon the nature and severity of the offence, the school administration reserves the right to suspend or expel the students immediately.

Teenagers' complaints made on social media about teachers, staff, or administrators may be interpreted as highly inappropriate or possibly a threat, and may be grounds for expulsion.

The policy used by the Nevada school may seem harsh. It isn't. Cyber bullying, like bullying without social media, is severely detrimental to the physical and psychological health of the victims. Some never recover. Victims have reported symptoms similar to post-traumatic stress disorder. Bullying crosses all social strata. It is our responsibility as a community to put an end to bullying of all kinds, one household at a time.

Parents should be aware of cyber bullying, cyber stalking, identity theft, and the effect these have on people of any age. Make your teenagers aware that email, text messages, and shared online images can cause embarrassment or be perceived as a threat. These messages are easily forwarded and, by altering their meaning, cause distress to the sender and recipient. Explain that friends and family may be the victims and might be harassed. Sometimes bullying starts with online friendships (Cox Communications, 2006).

Warning Signs That Someone May Be the Victim of Cyber Bullying

- Changes in mood, behavior, sleep, or appetite
- Depression or anxiety
- Crying for no reason
- Falling behind in homework
- Withdrawal from friends/activities
- Avoidance of school or group gatherings

How Parents Can Help:

- Talk to your child regularly.
- Tell your child not to respond to online comments.
- Don't threaten to take away your child's technology.
- Report the behavior to teachers, parents, police, and online service providers.
- Save, print out, and document evidence of cyber bullying (Rio Salado College, 2014).
- Remind your children to keep their passwords to themselves.

Even if children trust their friends, loyalties change, and there is always a risk of your child's social media account getting hacked. Teach children to think before they press the send key. Have them read what they've written a few times first and perhaps wait until the next day to send it. Once information is sent to the internet, it stays there. Google has a safety center online that has several useful videos about staying cyber safe. For more information, visit stopbullying.gov/cyberbullying. You can report illegal online activity to the Internet Crime Complaint Center: http://www.ic3.gov.

Ignoring the problem won't make it go away. Be alert and aware. Cyber bullying affects us all.

References for Adolescence

American Academy for Pediatrics. (10/28/2013). Managing media: We need a plan. Retrieved from www.aap.org/en-us/about-the-aap/aap-press-room/Pages/Managing-Media-We-Need-a-Plan. aspx#sthash.L2zpPhOF.dpuf.

Buikema, Daniel. Director of Guidance (08/2013 and 04/2014). Interviews: cyber bullying.

Christoff, K., Gordon, A. M., Smallwood, J., Smith, R., & Schooler, J. W. (3/27/2009). Experience sampling during fMRI reveals default network and executive system contributions to mind wandering. *Proceedings of the National Academy of Sciences of the United States of America.* Retrieved from http://www.pnas.org/content/early/2009/05/11/0900234106.full.pdf+html.

Current internet facts (2008). Cox Communications tween internet safety survey, Wave II - in partnership with the National Center for Missing & Exploited Children (NCMEC) and John Walsh (2006). Retrieved from http://www.scag.gov/wp-content/uploads/2011/03/wwkfacts2.pdf

Ford, John, DDS (04/2014). Interview: dangers to health due to bulimia.

Gupta, A. (4/07/2009). The interesting connection between math and music. *The Vancouver Sun.* Retrieved from http://www.vancouversun.com/Entertainment/interesting+connection+between+math+music/1473881/story.html

Helfinstein, S. M., & Poldrack, R. (2012). The young and the reckless. *Nature Neuroscience, 15*(6), 803-804.

Ho, Y. C., Cheung, M. C., & Chan, A. S. (2003). Music training improves verbal but not visual memory: cross-sectional and longitudinal explorations in children. *Neuropsychology, 17*(3), 439-500.

Lockwood, D. H., Heffner, T. C., DiGirolamo, M., Harp, J., & Stevens, J. (2000). Obesity: Pathology and therapy. *Handbook of Experimental Pharmacology, 149,* 3-28.

NOBullying.com (2012). Six unforgettable cyberbullying cases. Retrieved from http://nobullying.com/six-unforgettable-cyber-bullying-cases and http://www.ryanpatrickhalligan.org.

Phi Theta Kappa Honor Society, Rio Salado College (12/2013). *Help stop cyber bullying*. Retrieved from http://www.riosalado.edu/about/teaching-learning/student-life/PhiThetaKappa/Documents/cyber_bullying_final_Jan2014.pdf

Salimkhan, G., Manago, A., & Greenfield, P. (2010). The construction of the virtual self on MySpace. *Cyberpsychology: Journal of Psychosocial Research on Cyberspace, 4*(1). http://cyberpsychology.eu/view.php?cisloclanku=2010050203&article=1.

Selemon, L. D. (2013). A role for synaptic plasticity in the adolescent development of executive function. *Translational Psychiatry, 3*(3), e238. Retrieved from http://www.nature.com or doi:10.1038/tp.2013.7

Sleep in adolescents (13 to 18 years) (n.d.). Adapted from Mindell, J. A., & Owens, J.A. (2003). *A Clinical guide to pediatric sleep: Diagnosis and management of sleep problems*. Philadelphia, PA: Lippincott Williams & Wilkins. Retrieved from http://www.nationwidechildrens.org.

Spear, L. P. (2000). The adolescent brain and age-related behavioral manifestations. *Neuroscience and Behavioral Psychology, 24*(4), 417-463.

Steinberg, L. (1989). Impact of puberty on family relations: Effects of puberty status and puberty timing. *Developmental Psychology, 23*(3), 451-460.

Steinberg, L. (11/27/2013). Adapted from Henry and Bryna David Lecture, 10/03/2011. Should the science of adolescent brain development inform public policy? *Issues in Science and Technology*. Retrieved from http://issues.org/28-3/steinberg/.

Toma, John J. (07/2014 and 08/2014). Interviews, child development.

Woolston, W. (October 2008). Do "great expectations" matter? The relationship between teacher expectations and student academic success. Presentation for: The Institute for Research on Education Policy & Practice, Stanford University, Stanford, California.

Adolescence Further Reading

AFP/Reuters. (2/26/2008). Aggressive teens have mismatched brains. *ABC Science*. Retrieved from http://www.abc.net.au/science/articles/2008/02/26/2173061.htm.

Body image and advertising to youth. (06/21/2011). American Medical Association. Retrieved from http://www.ama-assn.org/ama/pub/news/news/all-new-policies.page.

Blakemore, S. J., & Choudhury, S. (2006). Development of the adolescent brain: Implications for executive function and social cognition. *Journal of Child Psychology and Psychiatry, 47*(3), 296-312.

Buikema, Daniel, Director of Guidance, practice in Las Vegas, Nevada.

Carasco, J. (2008). Common geometry formulas. Retrieved from http://www.basic-mathematics.com/common-geometry-formulas.html.

Crome, J. (n.d.). Geometry park: Teaching angles, triangles, and polygons. Retrieved from http://www.songsforteaching.com/geometryparkusa/geometrypark.htm.

Campbell, I. G., Higgins, L. M., Trinidad, J. M., Richardson, P., & Feinberg, I. (2007). The increase in longitudinally measured sleepiness across adolescence in related to the maturational decline in low-frequency EEG power. *Sleep, 30*(12), 1677-1688. Department of Psychiatry and Behavioral Sciences, University of California, Davis Sleep Lab. Retrieved from http://www.journalsleep.org/ViewAbstract.aspx?pid=27006.

Dakin, P. (2/24/2014). Social media affecting teen's concepts of friendship, intimacy. *CBC News: Health*. Retrieved from http://www.cbc.ca/news/health/social-media-affecting-teens-concepts-of-friendship-intimacy-1.2543158.

Devlin, K. (2000). The math gene: How mathematical thinking evolved and why numbers are like gossip. New York, NY: Basic Books.

Ford, John, DDS, private practice, Chicago area.

Gislason, S. (2011). *The human brain in health and disease: Adolescent brain*. British Columbia, Canada: Persona Digital Books.

Goudarzi, S. (9/07/2006). Study: Why teens don't care. *livescience*. Retrieved from http://www.livescience.com/7151-study-teens-care.html.

Gupta, A. (3/11/2009). Math is omnipresent and beautiful. *The Vancouver Sun*. Retrieved from http://www.mprime.ca/sites/default/files/News/Media Coverage/2009/Math Matters_March_April 2009/MathMatters_full series.pdf.

Internet Crime Complaint Center. http://www.ic3.gov.

Kruszelnicki, K. S. (10/12/2009). Juggling rewires the brain. *ABC Science*. Retrieved from http://www.abc.net.au/science/articles/2009/10/12/2711305.htm.

Kruszelnicki, K. S. (5/03/2007). Teenage sleep. *ABC Science*. Retrieved from http://www.abc.net.au/science/articles/2007/05/03/1913123.htm.

Lavelle, P. (7/29/2003). Music improves language and memory. *ABC Science*. Retrieved from http://www.abc.net.au/science/articles/2003/07/29/911523.htm.

LiveScience Staff (5/17/2005). Why teens are lousy at chores. *livescience*. Retrieved from http://www.livescience.com/270-teens-lousy-chores.html.

Managing media: We need a plan (10/28/2013). American Academy of Pediatrics. Retrieved from http://www.aap.org/en-us/about-the-aap/aap-press-room/Pages/Managing-Media-We-Need-a-Plan.aspx.

Moskowitz, C. (3/23/2009). Teen brains clear out childhood thoughts. *LiveScience*. Retrieved from http://www.livescience.com/3435-teen-brains-clear-childhood-thoughts.html.

Pain, C. (4/02/2012). Teen brains undergo neural pruning. *ABC Science*. Retrieved from http://www.abc.net.au/science/articles/2012/04/02/3467743.htm?site=sc&topic=latest.

Peer pressure: Its influence on teens and decision making (2008). *Scholastic*. Retrieved from http://headsup.scholastic.com/articles/peer-pressure-its-influence-on-teens-and-decision-making.

Rich, M. (n.d.). *1.0 Virtual sexuality: The influence of entertainment media on sexual attitudes and behavior*. May download pdf from e-bookspdf.org. Retrieved from https://thenationalcampaign.org/sites/default/files/resource-supporting-download/mm_1.0.pdf.

Rimalower, L. (n. d.). MySpace, yourspace, ourspace? Helping teens safety navigate online identity. LaFamily.com. Retrieved from http://www.lafamily.com/parenthood/parenting-postmodern-teen/myspace-yourspace-ourspace-helping-teens-safely-navigate-online.

Rimalower, L. (n.d.). *Parenting the postmodern teen: Stopping photoshop from cropping self-esteem*. LAFamily.com Retrieved from http://www.lafamily.com/parenthood/parenting-postmodern-teen/stopping-photo-shop-cropping-self-esteem.

Salleh, A. (11/27/2000). Sleep improves memory. *ABC Science Online*. Retrieved from http://www.abc.net.au/science/articles/2000/11/27/216359.htm.

Sleep and teens. (n.d.). UCLA Sleep Disorder Center. *UCLA Health*. Retrieved from http://sleepcenter.ucla.edu/body.cfm?id=63.

Steinberg, L. (11/27/2013). Adapted from Henry and Bryna David Lecture, 10/03/2011. Should the science of adolescent brain development inform public policy? *Issues in Science and Technology*. Retrieved from http://issues.org/28-3/steinberg/.

Sohn, E. (5/18/2010). Teen brain wired to take risks. *ABC Science*. Retrieved from http://www.abc.net.au/science/articles/2010/05/18/2902619.htm.

Toma, John J. Ph.D. Neuropsychology. Biltmore Evaluation and Treatment Services. Phoenix.

Vani, N. (2014). *Adam and Eve Hit the Gym*. Retrieved from http://truestarhealth.com/members/cm_archives11ML3P1A19.html.

Voice of America (11/02/2009). Study shows brain's problem-solving function at work while we daydream. Retrieved from http://www.voanews.com/content/a-13-2009-05-20-voa28-68786577/411090.html.

Wallace, K. (10/30/2013). Forget TV! iPhones and iPads dazzle babies. *CNN Living: CNN Parents*. Retrieved from http://www.cnn.

com/2013/10/29/living/parents-babies-kids-screen-time-guidelines/index.html.

Wolfe, P. (09/2011). *The adolescent brain: A work in progress*. Retrieved from http://patwolfe.com/2011/09/the-adolescent-brain-a-work-in-progress/.

Section 5

Siblings and Divorce— Infants through Adolescence

The following chapters, "Siblings" and "Divorce," pertain to all ages discussed in this book, so they are set apart from the other topics.

Siblings

Bringing Home Baby

Some children accept change and welcome a new sibling, gently touching the baby's fingers and toes. They talk to their new brother or sister in "Parentese," a higher-pitched musical voice, using short sentences and enjoy the baby's presence. Other children have difficulty adjusting to life with a new sibling.

> Mr. and Mrs. Yarnell brought home their new daughter, Hazel, and introduced her to their three other children. The two oldest children greeted the new baby first, happy to see her. Then the once-youngest child in

> the Yarnell family met her sister. Donna, age two, was angry. She did not want a baby sister.
>
> Mrs. Yarnell sat down on a living room chair so their daughter would have easy access to the new baby. "Come closer, Donna. Say hello to your baby sister."
>
> Donna clenched her fists and shook her head violently back and forth. She was having none of the baby. *She* was the baby, not this red squirmy thing in a pink blanket.
>
> "Donna, what's wrong with you? Come and say hello to Hazel." Mr. Yarnell motioned for Donna to come closer.
>
> Donna walked to her mother, fists still clenched, and punched baby Hazel in the face.
>
> Horrified at the action of his daughter, Mr. Yarnell was speechless.
>
> Mrs. Yarnell's face turned pale. "Donna, you are in time out!"

Preparing Siblings for the New Baby

Change is difficult for most people. A new sibling alters a family. Arrangements of space in the home, times for meals, and lack of parental energy disrupt the accustomed daily flow of family life. Communication between family members about the coming changes is critical.

The timing of discussions about the pregnancy with children will depend upon their age and maturity. Young children have no sense of time. It will make more sense to a preschooler that his new sibling will arrive, for example, when the seasons change (Sibling Relationships, 2014).

> Four-year-old Oscar looked at his mother's distended belly. "Mommy, when is the baby coming?"
>
> "Oscar, do you remember those flowers that need ants to help them open?"
>
> "Uh huh, peeneez. The ants go all over them.

> Peeneez smell good!"
> "That's right, they do smell wonderful. When the peonies open up, it will be time for the baby to come."
> Oscar climbed onto his mother's lap and put his hand on her belly. "What is it, Mommy?"
> "It's either a boy or a girl. We won't know until the baby is born. You like surprises, don't you, Oscar?"
> "I wanna horse."

According to kidshealth.com, the following activities may encourage positive feelings in preparation for a new baby:

- Going through your child's baby pictures
- Reading books about childbirth (make sure they're developmentally appropriate)
- Visiting friends who have infants
- Packing a bag for the hospital
- Thinking of potential baby names
- Going to the doctor to hear the baby's heartbeat

Set aside time for the older children to have one-to-one time with Mom or Dad while the baby sleeps. Quality time is much more important than quantity. Time alone with a parent helps the older sibling feel special. This may help reduce resentment and anger towards the baby and lessen the probability of regression in younger siblings (baby talk or bed wetting), as well as poor behavior in the older siblings.

Sibling Rivalry

Sibling issues develop as soon as the newborn comes home. Sometimes jealousy begins before the baby is born. Children are accustomed to a certain level of attention. If that attention changes dramatically, the firstborn may show unusual signs of neediness, reverting to more baby-like behavior.

Age and temperament (mood, disposition, the ability to deal with change) of children determine the severity of sibling rivalry. Toddlers and younger preschoolers believe that any toy near them is theirs. If an older or younger sibling takes the toy away or is perceived to have taken it away, the toddler will act out. School-aged children have a strong sense of fairness, particularly when the object at stake is theirs. They will have trouble understanding that fair and equal do not mean the same thing. Teenagers, striving to be independent, may be resentful of extra responsibilities placed on them. *"Why do I have to do all the babysitting? It's not fair!"*

If the household is one where the adults communicate well and resolve problems using non-aggressive methods, the children in the household will be more likely to solve their own issues using similar non-aggressive methods—a good habit for life.

Older children should have the opportunity to resolve problems on their own. Teenagers have a strong need to be independent. Mom and Dad will not always be there to mediate.

> Gordon and Lloyd, ages fourteen and twelve, respectively, shared a large bedroom in the attic of their parents' house. Both boys were intelligent and enjoyed their privacy.
>
> Gordon liked a neat, orderly room. Lloyd let things drop to the floor and created piles of clothing, books, and leftover food wrappers all over the room.
>
> Gordon had enough. "Lloyd, get your crap off the floor. This looks like a pigsty."
>
> "What? It's my room, too. If I wanna throw my stuff around, too bad for you."
>
> Gordon gave Lloyd a withering glance and stormed out. Lloyd sat on his bed, put his headphones on, and let the music muffle the sound of Gordon's loud grumbling as he walked down the hall.
>
> Gordon returned with masking tape. "Listen, I'm dividing . . . are you hearing me?" He stomped over to Lloyd who was reclining on his bed, eyes closed, headphones cradling his ears. Gordon lifted half the headphone off Lloyd's head. "Now can you hear me?"

> "What's your problem, Gordon?"
>
> "This mess! I'm gonna measure the room to make sure we each have half. Then I'll mark it with tape. You don't throw your stuff on my side. I don't complain about yours."
>
> The tape solution helped Gordon deal with Lloyd's clutter. He felt a need to annoy his brother. He wished Lloyd's inner slob would neaten up.
>
> Each of the brothers had a window on their respective halves of the room. Gordon liked to sleep in a room with a cool temperature. Lloyd preferred warmth. The early fall season approached with cool nights. Gordon opened his window wide to let in the night air.
>
> Lloyd woke up in the early hours of the morning, shivering. "Gordon, close your window. I'm freezing!"
>
> Gordon sat up in bed and smiled at his younger brother. "I like my side of the room to be colder. Deal with it."
>
> Since the disagreement never came to blows, both parents bowed out of the quarrel. The only requests their parents had were that whatever happened in their room stayed in their room, that they keep the racket to a minimum, and no bloodshed.
>
> Eventually, Lloyd made a deal with Gordon. The window on Gordon's side would remain open a crack, and Lloyd would pile his stuff neatly in separate crates.

Non-aggressive methods of problem solving keep rivalry in check for more than siblings' issues at home. It is helpful in school and playground situations for children and the work environment for adolescents and adults. When adults resolve problems using non-aggressive methods and communicate well, children will mirror their parents' behavior. Thinking a problem through to a peaceful resolution is the best for all.

Divorce

When people marry and take their wedding vows, they believe their marriage will last. Lives change. People's needs and wants sometimes differ, to the point where being together is no longer desirable or recommended. In some cases, it is mutually agreed; the couples were better friends than married partners. The two may remain friendly, or at least somewhat civil.

Often both parties are not in agreement, and bickering, or worse, ensues. If there are children involved, tension between parents is felt sharply by all members of the family. Anger between parents may be so pervasive and overwhelming that children's feelings of distress may not be noticed by their parents.

Take a deep breath, step back from the emotional tornado, and find a way to speak with your estranged spouse. All children feel stressed throughout the process of divorce—before, during, and after. Preteens, ten- through twelve-year-olds, and preschoolers have the most difficult time dealing with divorce (Amato, 1994; Johnson, 2014).

Behavior Changes

Children who are egocentric—who feel the world revolves around them—have a very difficult time with divorce, as they feel it is their fault the parents are separating. It is normal for children of divorcing parents to feel anxious, angry, and depressed.

Those children who witness threats to a caregiver are more likely to exhibit fear, aggressive behavior, and increased tension than exposure to other kinds of trauma (Scheeringa & Zeanah, 1995).

All children are affected differently, depending upon gender, age, position in family—whether the oldest, middle, or youngest, and by emotional closeness or distance from each parent. A parent's ability to distance emotions about the divorce from their relationship to their children also makes a difference in how well the children weather the divorce.

Children need guidance. They need to know that, whatever happens between their parents, it is not their fault. Parents who work out a plan to discuss what is happening and the upcoming changes have less stressed children. Any change causes stress; it is a matter of degree.

Fear of the unknown is a huge issue for children.

- What will be different?
- Where will I live?
- With whom will I live?
- Do I need to change schools?
- Will I see my friends?

There may be changes in behavior at home, as well as at school. Younger children past bedwetting stage may regress and begin wetting the bed at night. This is embarrassing for them and is not something they do out of anger towards parents. This regression is a reaction to stress. Young children, in particular preschool-aged, may become anal retentive (holding bowel movements for more than two days). These children feel their lives spinning out of control. They can control their bowels if nothing else, at least for a while.

Children of all ages may have more difficulty in school. Their attention is back at home, not learning in class.

> Ten-year-old Ella sat at a desk near the window towards the back of the classroom. The spot was perfect. She could sit and stare out the window, listen to the rain fall, watch the snow slide off the building next door, or see birds soar. How she wished she were a bird. She wanted to fly away.
> "Ella, what do you think the answer is?"
> "I'm sorry, Miss Martin. I didn't hear your question."
> "You need to pay attention, Ella. Participation is part of your grade."

"Yes, ma'am. Could you repeat the question, please?"

At home, Ella's parents argued nonstop. Homework had become impossible with all the yelling, so her grades slipped. She knew she was bright and should be doing better in school, but she decided it was smarter to remain quiet and try to blend in with the walls rather than to ask for help. Once, a friend called Ella's house during dinner time to explain how to do a math problem. Ella's father screamed at her to get off the phone and get back to dinner. Ella lied to her friend, saying she understood what to do in order to get off the phone quickly. One parent screaming led to both parents screaming. She hated the noise.

Later in the evening, Ella noticed her mother's eyes were red-rimmed and puffy. She was holding a soggy tissue in her hand. Ella finally asked her mother if she and her father were getting divorced.

"What made you ask that, Ella?"

"You and Daddy are always yelling."

"No, Ella, we aren't getting divorced. All mommies and daddies yell."

Ella understood what her mother said but knew that not all parents screamed as often as hers did.

Children's Positive Adjustment

"Although divorce is painful for children, remaining in a high-conflict intact family is worse than making the transition to a low-conflict, single parent household. . . . When divorcing parents put aside their disagreements and support one another in their child-rearing roles, children have the best chance of growing up competent, stable, and happy" (Berk, 2002, p. 508).

Around 80 percent of children show an improved adjustment two years after the divorce. Some have serious difficulties through adulthood.

The biggest factors to children's positive adjustment are:

- Handling stress—how the custodial parent deals with the stress of divorce. No one should go this alone. If family is unable or unwilling to assist, talk to friends or others of trust in the community.
- Shelter the children from conflict. Children notice everything. Parents cannot hide what is going on, but they can use common sense and keep tempers down.
- Use of an Authoritative parenting style, which stresses warmth and consistency of discipline, helps children withstand the stressors of divorce and have fewer adjustment problems (Berk, 2002).

> Michael, age eight, rarely saw his father, Donald, who was often away at work. When Donald tried to speak to his son, Michael stared at his father and barely spoke. Michael felt little connection with his father.
>
> Michael's mother, Gloria, tried to explain to Donald that Michael did not know what to say to someone he rarely interacted with.
>
> Donald's job became all-consuming. He had no time for his family. The job supplied financial support for his wife and son but no emotional support. Money buys things but doesn't supply love.
>
> Gloria attempted to get her husband to try family counseling. He was uninterested, feeling nothing was wrong with the cushy life he provided. Crushed, she filed for divorce and moved Michael out of the only home he ever knew.
>
> They relocated to a small apartment above a grocery store in a busy area of town. Gloria chose to stay in the town Michael grew up in, so he could attend the

> same school, despite an opportunity to move in with her sister twenty miles away.
>
> Donald felt like his wife snatched his son and moved away for no reason. He got angry; he felt she was crazy to leave such a soft life. He decided to get back at Gloria for leaving him. He would play her son against her and buy Michael's love if necessary. He would get his son back and break Gloria's heart, as she had hurt him.
>
> Michael spoke with a friend at school. "They want me to choose, but whatever I do, someone will be hurt or mad. Dad has been so nice lately, but my mom . . . I just can't decide."

This scenario may be reversed: a child staying with dad, where mom is estranged. Misunderstandings abound during times of great stress and conflict.

"What I Need From My Mom and Dad": A Child's List of Wants

- I need both of you to stay involved in my life. Please write letters, send email, make phone calls, and ask me lots of questions. When you don't stay involved, I feel like I'm not important, and you don't really love me.
- Please stop fighting, and work hard to get along with each other. Try to agree on matters related to me. When you fight about me, I think I did something wrong, and I feel guilty.
- I want to love you both and enjoy the time I spend with you. Please support me in sharing that time. If you act jealous or upset, I feel like I need to take sides and love one parent more than the other.
- Please communicate directly with my other parent, so I don't have to carry messages back and forth.
- When talking about my other parent, please say only nice things or don't say anything at all. When you say mean,

unkind things about my other parent, I feel like you expect me to take your side.
- Please remember that I want both of you to be a part of my life. I count on my mom and dad to raise me, to teach me what is important, and to help me when I have problems.

(Kemp, Smith, & Segal, 2013, Source: University of Missouri)

Therapy Types

Counseling helps children cope with the family transitions caused by separation and divorce. Psychologists, social workers, and others have been specifically trained to work with children during times of stress and transitions of all kinds. Some schools offer after school in house programs for children dealing with family changes. Counseling is available through some workplaces. No one lives in a vacuum. The stress family members feel follows them everywhere, making concentration difficult and tempers short.

Younger children use play and art to express their feelings. Many times they need to communicate what is happening to them internally but are unable to do so at home for fear of causing more problems in an already stressed environment. Children need to vent their feelings. Reading stories and talking about what happens to the characters in a book may help children relate with and state their own feelings.

Older children need to talk to someone who is not directly involved with problems at home. They can express their feelings more openly with other children going through stressful situations and with adults trained to listen empathetically. Talking therapy, dramatizations of stories, art, or a combination of therapies are valuable methods to help children work through their feelings. Counseling is not preaching. There is no blame. Counseling help children better cope with their emotions and feelings.

People fall in and out of love. As we evolve in our humanity, we don't always grow closer to each other. When a marriage dies and divorce is inevitable, children need to know they are not being cut off or out of either parent's life. A marriage died—not the people in it.

Parenting... A Work in Progress

Children deserve love. They are not responsible for the divorce. As difficult as it may be for the divorcing adults, those children fortunate enough to have parents who manage to remain civil and handle divorce proceedings with empathy towards their children have the best chance of growing up to be happy, stable adults.

Children's Books on Divorce

(List courtesy of DeBord, 1984)

For Preschoolers and Early Elementary

All about Divorce, by Mary Blitzer Field
Always, Always, by Crescent Dragonwagon
Annie Stories: A Special Kind of Storytelling, by Judith S. Wallerstein and Doris Brett.
Dinosaurs Divorce: A Guide toChanging Families, by Laurene and Marc Brown
Free to Be . . . A Family: A Book About All Kinds Of Belongings, by Marlo Thomas
Why Are We Getting a Divorce? by Peter Mayle
Daddy Doesn't Live Here Anymore, by R. Turaw
Months of Sundays, by R. Blue

For Adolescent and Early Teens

Angel Face, by Norma Klein. For ages 12 and up. Presented from a boy's point of view.
The Divorce Express, by Paula Danziger. For ages 12 and up. Presented from a girl's point of view.
Free to Be . . . A Family: A Book About All Kinds Of Belongings, by Marlo Thomas
How It Feels When Parents Divorce, by Jill Krementz
It's Not the End of the World, by Judy Blume
Talking about Divorce: A Dialogue Between Parent and Child, by Ead Groliman
What's Going to Happen to Me? When Parents Separate or Divorce, by Eda LeShan

Divorce, by A. Gruasell
When Mom and Dad Divorce, by S. Nickman
How to Get It Together When Your Parents Are Coming Apart, by A. K. Richards and I. Willis

References for Siblings and Divorce

Amato, P. (1994). Life-span adjustment of children to their parents' divorce. *Children and divorce, 4*(1). Los Altos, CA: Packard Foundation.

DeBord, K. (1994). Children and divorce. *The Future of Children, 4*(1). Center for the Future of Children. The David and Lucile Packard Foundation. Retrieved from http://futureofchildren.org/futureofchildren/publications/docs/04_01_FullJournal.pdf.

Berk, L. (2002). Infants, Children, and Adolescents. Boston, MA: Allyn & Bacon.

Johnson, M. (2014). What age is the most difficult for a child to endure a divorce? *Everyday Life*. Demand Media. Retrieved from http://everydaylife.globalpost.com/age-difficult-child-endure-divorce-19920.html.

Kemp, G., Smith, M., & Segal, J. (12/2013). HELPGUIDE.org. Retrieved from http://www.helpguide.org/mental/children_divorce.htm.

Preparing your child for a new sibling. Nemours. Retrieved from http://kidshealth.org/parent/emotions/feelings/sibling_prep.html.

Scheeringa, M. S., & Zeanah, C. H. (1995). Symptom expression and trauma variables in children under 48 months of age. *Infant Mental Health Journal, 16*(4), 259-270. Retrieved from http://www.researchgate.net/publication/230127107_Symptom_expression_and_trauma_variables_in_children_under_48_months_of_age.

Sibling Relationships. (5/08/2014). American Academy of Pediatrics. Healthychildren.org. Retrieved from http://www.healthychildren.org/English/ages-stages/prenatal/Pages/Preparing-Your-Family-for-a-New-Baby.aspx.

The First Weeks Home: Easing the New Sibling Transition. Nemours. Retrieved from http://kidshealth.org/parent/emotions/feelings/sibling_prep.html

Further Reading

Fabricius, W. V., & Luecken, L. J. (2007). Postdivorce living arrangements, parent conflict, and long-term physical health correlates for children of divorce. *Journal of Family Psychology, 21*(2), 195-205. Retrieved from http://www.ncbi.nlm.nih.gov/pubmed/17605542.

Katz, L. (1979). Brotherhood/Sisterhood begin at home: Notes on sibling rivalry. Chicago, IL: Education Resource Information Center. Retrieved from http://files.eric.ed.gov/fulltext/ED194191.pdf.

Lowery, C. R., & Settle, S. A. (1985). Effects of divorce on children: Differential effect of custody and visitation patterns. *Family Relations, 34*(4). Minneapolis, MN: National Council on Family Relations. Retrieved from http://www.jstor.org/discover/10.2307/584005?uid=3739552&uid=2129&uid=2&uid=70&uid=4&uid=3739256&sid=21104593737677.

Parenting... A Work in Progress

Conclusion

People
Are
Really
Entering
New
Territory

What would the perfect parent look like?

Perfect consumes no suspect additives, always gets enough sleep, and never feels stressed. Perfect understands precisely the meaning of each sound Baby produces, making crying unnecessary. Perfect prepares and freezes homemade organic meals for the week. That way Perfect never has to leave Baby in an infant swing for an extended time while preparing meals.

Perfect never suffers from a loss of self-control in any situation, including trips to the grocery store when Toddler rips open a bag of cookies at the checkout counter.

Parenting... A Work in Progress

Perfect always has the best suggestions for dealing with childhood drama and never overfills Grade-schooler's schedule with too many extracurricular activities, providing the perfect balance of education and recreation.

The Perfects have meals together every morning and evening and discuss the current events of each family member's life during the relaxed meals.

Guess what? Children don't require perfection. They need to learn how to share, pay attention, communicate, and express love. These four important qualities must be modeled for children to emulate.

Parenting is difficult work. Treating each child in the household equally does not guarantee they'll react the same way. All children, even within the same family, are different from one another. With each new child come new and exciting experiences. Parents really are people entering new territory, with each new member changing the family dynamic.

Who hasn't felt guilty for not giving enough time to or having enough money for their children? Remember, quality time is more important than quantity time. Pay attention to children now, and they will listen to you later. Their parents' attention is more important than any amount of money.

Breathe deeply, slowly.
Smile often.
Enjoy the children.
Time passes quickly.

About the Author

Ellen Buikema is a parent and former teacher. A graduate of the University of Illinois at Chicago, she received her M.Ed. specializing in Early Childhood. She has extensive post-graduate studies in special education from Northeastern Illinois University and has published short stories and poetry. This is her first book. She lives outside Phoenix with her husband and two dogs. Learn more about her at www.ellenbuikema.com.

www.ingramcontent.com/pod-product-compliance
Lightning Source LLC
Chambersburg PA
CBHW031414290426
44110CB00011B/380